T0170330

DIFFUSION RESEARCH IN RURAL SOCIOLOGY

The Record and Prospects for the Future

FREDERICK C. FLIEGEL

With PETER F. KORSCHING

Foreword by James J. Zuiches

Social Ecology Press
Middleton • Wisconsin

Publisher's Cataloging-in-Publication
(Provided by Quality Books, Inc.)

Fliegel, Frederick C.
     Diffusion research in rural sociology : the record
and prospects for the future / Frederick C. Fliegel with
Peter F. Korsching. -- 1st Social Ecology Press ed.
     p. cm.
     Includes bibliographical references and index.
     LLC 92-19426
     ISBN: 0-941042-31-6

     1. Agriculture--Technology transfer. 2. Diffusion of.
innovations. 3. Agricultural innovations.
4. Sociology, Rural. 5. Agriculture--Technology transfer--
Research. 6. Diffusion of innovations--Research.
I. Korsching, Peter F. II. Title.

S494.5.15F65 2001   338.1'6'072
                                           QBI01-700724

First Social Ecology Press edition published in 2001
Previously published in 1993 by Greenwood Press, Inc

Social Ecology Press ™
P.O. Box 620863
Middleton, Wisconsin 53562-0863, USA
Phone: 1-888-364-3277

Printed in the United States of America on recycled paper
10 9 8 7 6 5 4 3 2 1

Contents

Contents

Figures and Tables

TABLES

Preface
To the Second Edition

It was fitting that the Rural Sociological Society's Fiftieth Anniversary Series included a volume on diffusion research in rural sociology, and that Frederick Fliegel, who had a prominent role in the development of this area of scholarship, authored the volume. For many years it was a dominant area of scholarship in rural sociology and it helped to establish the discipline's position and legitimacy in the land grant system. Over the last three decades diffusion research relinquished its dominance to the point that today it is a very minor player in the discipline. But Fliegel's statement in the preface to the first edition, that the diffusion research tradition in rural sociology remains viable, continues to be valid.

There is no denying that scholarly research by rural sociologists on the diffusion of innovations has declined. In his preface Fliegel documents the rise and decline of articles published in *Rural Sociology* that dealt with diffusion. I have not calculated the percent of diffusion related articles that have appeared in *Rural Sociology* over the last decade (1990 to present), but the number of articles can be counted on one hand. Additional articles by rural sociologists can be found in a variety of other journals, primarily those related to rural, development, and natural resource topics. Even so, the total number of contributions by rural sociologists to the diffusion literature pales in comparison to earlier years. In the chapter I contribute to this work I review the research literature that has appeared over the last decade following the volume's first publication, and I discuss some of the reasons that have been offered to explain this decline. Rogers (1995) believed that the decline resulted from the major theoretical and methodological issues of the model having been resolved. Ruttan (1996) felt that rural sociologists were too parochial and failed to embrace methodological advances of researchers in other disciplines such as geographers, economists, and technologists. Fliegel believed that reliance on survey research methods and overcompensation for

viii   Preface To Second Edition

concerns over inappropriate innovations and immutable social structures inhibited research. No doubt, each of these factors has significantly contributed to the decline of diffusion research by rural sociologist, but I would like to offer an additional factor that I believe also has had a substantial impact. I did not include this in my chapter because I have no systematic data to document my assertions. Discussions, conversations, and observations from over 20 years of work in this area, however, do lend support to my beliefs.

The diffusion of innovations model is one of the most successful models that sociology, and indeed the social sciences, have produced. There are limitations to the model's application, limitations which have not always been recognized or heeded, but within the parameters of these limitations the model works for a broad spectrum of innovations in a great variety of situations. It has seen wide application by policy and decision makers in both the public and private spheres. It is this success, particularly its enthusiastic adoption and use by the private sector, which has contributed significantly to the model being spurned by rural sociologists. The "diffusion," if you will, of the model to the agribusiness sector in the 1960s, to allow agricultural corporations to better market their products to farmers, was viewed by many rural sociologists as compromising scholarly ideals. When concern about perceived misuse of the model by agricultural corporations was reinforced by criticisms of its shortcomings -- the pro innovations bias, the individual blame bias, and the inequality of impacts (Rogers, 1995) -- many rural sociologists felt the model was sufficiently discredited that it should be abandoned.

In the Sociology Department at Iowa State University we have long had, not surprisingly with this being the birthplace, so to speak, of the traditional diffusion of innovations model, a graduate course on the diffusion of innovations. Because of my background and work in this area I have taught the course since the early 1980s. In recent years I have had suggestions to make the course "more relevant" by converting it to a sociology of technology course. Over the years I have broadened the subject matter of the course, but the primary content continues to be the diffusion of innovations. I believe, as did Fliegel, that the diffusion of innovations continues to be an important, appropriate, and viable research area for rural sociology.

In my chapter I have attempted to demonstrate that despite the criticisms of the model and the relatively few publications on the topic in recent years by rural sociologists, it is a viable, even exciting, research area. New methods and theories are being introduced, and substantive areas investigated that go beyond the farm practices and technologies of so much of traditional diffusion research. Two major directions emerge in this research. The first maintains a strong tie to the classic diffusion of innovations model and uses new research methods, analytical techniques, or explores new concepts and relationships to refine the model. In the second research direction the investigators maintain few, if any, ties with the classic model. Their work thus results in the development of new models or paradigms of innovation diffusion. It should also be noted that a substantial number of the exciting advances in research methods and theory are occurring not in rural sociology, but in the broader sociology discipline. The research of rural diffusion scholars could benefit from these advances. Should Rogers publish a fifth edition of his book and make a serious effort to incorporate the latest research literature, the volume may differ considerably from the first four editions.

In writing the new chapter I have attempted to use an approach and style similar to Fliegel. I will let the reader decide the degree to which I have succeeded in my goal. To follow in the footsteps and endeavor to contribute to the work of one of rural sociology's eminent scholars is a daunting undertaking. It is interesting to speculate what Fliegel might have thought and written about the developments and directions of diffusion research over the last decade, given his extensive knowledge and critical insight derived from having been one of the central contributors to the development of the classic model. My assessment is that he would be as positive about the current state of diffusion research and its future as when he wrote his preface to the original edition of this volume.

Peter F. Korsching

Foreword

The publication of this volume, *Diffusion Research in Rural Sociology: The Record and Prospects for the Future,* by Frederick Fliegel, brings to a conclusion the Fiftieth Anniversary Series of the Rural Sociological Society. When the society initiated this series and asked me to serve as editor, I never expected that from concept to final publication of five volumes would take nearly eight years. Yet the Fiftieth Anniversary Series is one of which we can be proud, and this final volume represents the culmination of a research career that has been at the core of rural sociology for over half of its existence as a society. Dr. Frederick Fliegel, know as Fritz to friends and colleagues worldwide, completed this manuscript just prior to his untimely death. As editor I had read and commented on earlier version and had solicited reviews from members of the RSS before submitting the manuscript to Greenwood Press. Subsequent evaluation by Greenwood Press was extremely positive, but they included a number of editorial and substantive recommendations for improvements. Efforts to generate a final revision by colleagues were not successful, and Greenwood Press was growing concerned over the passage of time since the original completion.

The Rural Sociological Society, however, owes a dept of gratitude and appreciation to Dr. George Butler, acquisitions editor for the social and behavioral sciences at Greenwood Press, for he provided both a renewed commitment and stimulus to finish Fritz's volume in 1992.

As I reflected on the required changes, and reread the manuscript one more time, I was again impressed by the depth of analysis, the insights he expressed, and the prescience Fritz showed about the future research on impact of new technologies. He proposes a renewed emphasis on the structural antecedents and consequences of adoption. Who gains? Who loses? What are the environmental consequences of new technologies? By linking the answers to these questions to public policy, he anticipated the current USDA research initiative in markets, trade, and policy. In fact, Fritz raised the banner of a socioecological perspective in such technology assessment. In the USDA call for proposals for 1992, a major new program was established in technology assessment: to determine the benefits and costs of adopting new products and production methods. Such research is to provide empirical estimates of the impacts – socioeconomic and ecological – of adopting new practices. Fritz also recommends that we extend our impact analysis beyond technology to institutional technology, such as credit systems, advisory services, and other innovative ways of managing the institution of society. If Fritz Fliegel were alive today, I suspect he would be submitting a proposal to the USDA National Research Initiative, Markets, Trade and Policy, to study the impacts of new technologies on social systems.

In 1988 Fritz was recognized by the RSS, as a Distinguished Rural Sociologist, for his research on diffusion and adoption of new technology. His research spanned the globe, including the United States, Japan, Brazil, India, and several African nations. As noted in the award document:

> His pioneering emphasis on the characteristics of technology has influenced thinking concerning agricultural development strategies so that, today, development planners consider the characteristics of technological packages before introducing them.
>
> From the beginning of his research career, Fritz always had a special interest in the consequences of new technology for small and low-resource farmers. His research strived to deal with obstacles low-resource farmers face in the agricultural development process, and the impacts of technological innovations on the farmers and their families. Fritz's research on the distribution effects of the "Green Revolution" in India is widely considered to be rural sociology's most sound

empirical contribution in this controversial area of
interpreting implemented change.

   Fritz made invaluable contributions to our
profession. He was an invaluable counselor and
consultant to younger rural sociologists. He held
numerous offices, including that of president, of our
Society. Fritz is the most frequently published author
in the history of *Rural Sociolog,* (Warland, 1988:
445).

   I cite this commendation because as a graduate student, when
I submitted my first refereed paper to *Rural Sociology,* its editor was
Fritz Fliegel. He influenced me profoundly by his positive
suggestions to reviewers' criticisms and his subsequent publication in
Rural Sociology of research from my M.A. thesis. It is a strange
coincidence that I find myself editing Fritz's last major manuscript.
In this task, I owe thanks and appreciation to Ellen Abell, A Ph.D.
candidate in sociology at Washington State University. Ellen Abell
provided the research assistance, the careful reading and assessment,
and the efficient summarization of recent literature, published since
1987. Lucy Kong provided unfailingly cheerful word processing
assistance as we finished the revisions on the manuscript.

   Fritz never intended for this volume to be comprehensive in
its literature review. He preferred a selective use of important
research to make his point. Our strategy was to check the
corroborating literature through 1987, and conduct a forward search
through 1992 on the topics he emphasized. The core journals, *Rural
Sociology, The Rural Sociologist, Sociologia Ruralis, Economic
Development and Cultural Change,* and *Studies in Comparative
International Development,* were reviewed. If recent studies did not
significantly affect his argument, I did not include them. In a few
sections, reviewers strongly encouraged elaboration of the argument,
and after reviewing the appropriate literature, I did so. In these cases,
I take responsibility for any failure to continue the lucid arguments
the author intended. I make this statement because *Diffusion
Research in Rural Sociology* is truly a personal synthesis and
statement by one of our most distinguished rural sociologists.

                                          James J. Zuiches

Preface

Why another effort to review the work on diffusion of innovations? One might posit at least two perspectives from which that type of question could arise. First, from perhaps the most obvious perspective, the considerable success of three successive editions of Everett Rogers' *Diffusion of Innovations* (1962, 1971, 1983) can serve as evidence that the topic of diffusion has been amply covered. I can think of no other area of interest in rural sociology that has been anywhere near as thoroughly reviewed and documented as that of diffusion. And second, from a quite different perspective, one might argue that research on the diffusion of innovations is a dead issue, that rural sociologists were mistaken in their (our) enthusiasm for work on the topic, and that new approaches to the technological change process are at hand. No less a personage than William Foote Whyte (1985) can find it "surprising" that I (Fliegel and van Es. 1983) could be party to pointing out some of the shortcomings of diffusion research – Whyte uses the term "failure" – and yet declare the research tradition to be viable after forty years.

   Why, then, another review of research on the diffusion of innovations? In my opinion one need seek no farther than a recent and excellent article by Gartrell and Gartrell (1985) to document one's argument that the diffusion research tradition in rural sociology remains viable. The article cited capitalizes on that tradition and addresses research issues of a more basic nature than the bulk of the work that comprises the tradition addressed. Which is to say, indirectly, that somewhat different questions are being asked currently than was the case a generation ago, but research continues. The issue of viability seems to hinge on the value positions taken by or attributed to those who engage in the debate. I take it as a given that sociological research on the diffusion of agricultural innovations is not value free. I think that it is clear that especially the early research on diffusion was conducted from the tacit posture that modern technology was good for agriculture and for the farmer. And I think that it is also clear that some critics of the research tradition reject what Ruttan (1983) has called an emerging science-based agriculture, viewing it as invariably (inevitably?) leading to environmental degradation and/or a progressive impoverishment of the least powerful segment of agriculture, the smallholder and the family farmer. Value positions cannot be ignored but, in my opinion, they need not deter one from using the best theory and technique one can muster to address research questions. Research on diffusion continues, some good work is being done, and thus I argue that the "tradition" remains viable.

But, to repeat the initial question one more time, why *another* review of research on diffusion? In my opinion, Rogers has done a first-rate job of summarizing the very extensive diffusion research literature. By clearly defining concepts and presenting a long series of middle-range generalizations, Rogers has made the diffusion literature accessible to a far wider audience than would have been possible via the many separate research reports alone. The very success of Rogers' work also involves a trade-off, however. Much of the current familiarity with diffusion research stems from familiarity with Rogers' books alone. Ease of access to the literature does not necessarily assure penetration of the literature. Such penetration is in any case a formidable task because the literature is extensive. I think that a much less comprehensive review than that undertaken by Rogers, a review restricted to rural sociology and research on the diffusion of agricultural innovations, can be useful. If such a less ambitious review can focus on key issues from the perspective of rural sociology, and if such a review can at least illustrate if not penetrate the theoretical and technical issues which characterize the literature, then the utility I hope for will have been demonstrated.

The review articles occasioned by the recent completion of fifty years of publication of *Rural Sociology* make it an easy task to document trends in rural sociological research. Christenson and Garkovich (1985:512) report that but 0.4 percent of all articles in *Rural Sociology* dealt with diffusion in the 1936-45 period. By 1966-75 this proportion had increased to 8.2 percent of all articles, and then declined to 5.4 percent in the 1976-85 period.

In Part I of this volume I will illustrate the kinds of studies on diffusion done during the decades of apparently increasing interest, roughly from 1940 to 1970. Then Part II covers some of the more recent trends. I will illustrate what I consider to be some of the key ideas explored over that considerable time span, thus my coverage of the literature will be far from complete and possibly somewhat arbitrary. Nevertheless, it is my intent to document the sequence of ideas explored and work toward an understanding of why such ideas were explored and what one can conclude from the research results. Finally, in the last chapter of this volume I will discuss issues that I consider unresolved at this point in time and worthy of research in the future.

I

HISTORICAL OVERVIEW: FROM THE 1940s TO THE 1970s

Part I of this volume describes the early work that influenced the direction of diffusion research, the gradual institutionalization of the classical approach to diffusion research, and the spread of diffusion research to countries outside of the United States. Chapter 1 begins by describing conceptual and methodological antecedents to diffusion research. The contributions of the cultural lag hypothesis, the "discovery" of diffusion as a patterned process, and sample survey methodology to the development and utilization of diffusion research are discussed. The formation of what became known as the classical diffusion paradigm is then reviewed through an examination of the Iowa State hybrid corn studies. Finally, Chapter 1 offers a perspective on the reasons for the growth and popularity of diffusion research among rural sociologists from the 1940s to 1970s.

The diffusion research of this time period is characterized by a linear, socio-psychological approach. Chapter 2 describes the classical model of approach to diffusion and its primary focus on the information transfer process. Agricultural diffusion research attempted to operationally define farmers' adoption behavior, identify information flows to the farmer, and determine those individual farmer characteristics that affected the transfer of information. The consensus on diffusion that emerged from a wide variety of studies tended to define the adoption of agricultural innovations in terms of an individual propensity to be innovative, to view the process of adoption as a series of stages of awareness of a particular innovation, and to conceptualize the antecedents of adoption behavior as situational and personal characteristics of the farmer. The discussion of the development of diffusion models and concepts in Chapter 2 makes apparent the assumptions underlying rural sociological research on the diffusion of farm innovations.

Historical Overview

In the post-WW II era, many of these assumptions came to be questioned. Population increases and concerns about the adequacy of the food supply prompted the transfer of technologies and the spread of diffusion research to other countries. Chapter 3 describes this development and the questions that diffusion research in the third world brought up about the assumptions made in the classic diffusion research model. The use of mass media, literacy, and the link between education and innovativeness in the third world stimulated questions about diffusion as a linear process. In addition, recognition of the variation in control of farm resources by third world farmers alerted diffusion researchers to the need to take into account social structural differences in their models. Consideration of these issues provoked a major shift in theoretical perspective, influencing diffusion research in ways that will be taken up in Part II.

The First Wave of Diffusion Research

SOME ANTECEDENTS

Diffusion of innovations refers to the spread of innovations through a population. Diffusion is ordinarily thought of as the result of a number of individual or group adoption decisions, the aggregate result of being the spread of the innovation through a population. Research on the diffusion process by rural sociologists is commonly dated as starting with the Iowa State hybrid corn studies of the 1940s, beginning with Ryan and Gross (1943). There the intent was to better understand the diffusion of a particular innovation, hybrid corn, and later other innovations among Iowa farmers. I intend to discuss the Iowa studies in some detail, but before doing that I want to make at least brief reference to some earlier research and conceptualization that I think influenced the direction taken by what came to be a very popular research area.

William F. Ogburn is perhaps best known for his introduction of the "cultural lag hypothesis" (1922) to the sociological vocabulary. In its most abstract form the cultural lag hypothesis stipulated that two correlated elements of a culture might change at different rates, thereby setting up a situation I which a lesser degree of adjustment between the two elements might be perceived. The general idea is easy to illustrate: the development of the automobile, for example, made it apparent that many roads and city streets were quite inappropriate for the full utilization of the automobile's potential. Narrow roadways, sharp curves, steep grades, and rough or soft road surfaces all came to be viewed as problematic with respect to full use of the automobile. As a matter of fact, achieving some kind of reasonable accommodation between the automobile and the road system, problematic over fifty years ago, remains a problem today.

By and large development of automotive capacity and use has been viewed as a leading element in cultural change, and development of appropriate roadways has been viewed as lagging.

In a retrospective article on his own work, Ogburn (1957) proposed a formal addendum to the cultural lag hypothesis. Ogburn recognized that in recent world history the rapidity of technological change and its cumulative character tended to put technological change in the lead and make for an accumulation of lags in the non-technological realm of culture. He thus proposed that the more general form of the cultural lag hypothesis be preserved but that a technology-as-lead format of the hypothesis might be favored for work on current problems.

It is precisely the technology-as-lead variant of the cultural lag hypothesis that became important for diffusion research. The bulk of at least the early diffusion research took it for granted that technological innovations in agriculture were leading elements in cultural change. An array of non-technological (and often non-material) elements of culture – attitudes, values, social relationships, and so on – then represented the lagging elements. The primary objective of much of the early diffusion research was to determine which of the lagging elements were critical in delaying full acceptance of the leading (technological) elements.[1]

Some of the work of F. Stuart Chapin is also relevant as background to the discussion of diffusion research in agriculture. The particular point that I wish to make here is that Chapin (1928) documented what later came to be known as the "familiar S curve" of diffusion. Specifically, what Chapin (1928:369-384) demonstrated was that both the commission form of city government and the city manager form of government spread throughout the United States in a patterned manner. Acceptance was slow for a few years after first introduction. Then acceptance increased at a substantially higher rate for a time, and finally the rate of acceptance tapered off. When the frequency of adoption was plotted on a cumulative basis over time, the result was an S-shaped curve.[2]

I do not wish to suggest that Chapin made a "discovery" that directly influenced later diffusion research in rural sociology. My point is that thinking about diffusion as a clearly patterned process was extant in sociology before the research on agricultural innovations began. Furthermore, when later studies demonstrated that diffusion is a patterned process in many different contexts, I think that fact in itself attracted additional research attention to the area. As I will try to make clear later, the characteristic S curve of diffusion provided something of a framework for posing research questions (why the slow start, why two points of inflection in the curve, and so on) and added an element of coherence to the research effort.

Finally, I will mention here a diffusion study by a rural sociologist, Charles R. Hoffer (1942), which was published slightly before the first of the Iowa State reports. The Hoffer study can illustrate some of the antecedents within rural sociology of the later wave of diffusion research. Hoffer used an experimental design to determine whether an extension circular printed in English or in Dutch was more effective in persuading celery growers to adopt improved practices in western Michigan. A number of communities with significant numbers of smallholder celery growers of Dutch descent were first identified. A Dutch version of the circular was sent to growers in some of these communities, an English version was sent to growers in several others, and still others received neither version. A follow-up survey then determined that the circular had stimulated adoption of recommended practices and that the English version was more effective in stimulating adoption of innovations.

The specific results of the Hoffer study are of no direct interest here in that the findings were relevant to a small population. Several points are worthy of mention, however. First, the study can be viewed as representative of a body of work concerned with the effectiveness of pedagogical techniques. I will not review that work here but simply note the existence of research concerned with the process of technology transfer prior to the 1940s. Second, I find it intriguing that Hoffer used an experimental design while the later diffusion research tradition relied almost exclusively on the sample survey. I'm not sure what to make of that except to speculate that the sample survey was in fashion while experiments have never achieved that status among sociologists. And third, it is my opinion that the Hoffer study was largely ignored by later diffusion researchers because it focused on a specialty crop.[3] Hybrid corn was quite another matter, and I think it is fair to say that diffusion research became popular because it could ally itself with the dominant commercial approach of the larger agricultural research and development establishment. Having said that I turn now to the Iowa State studies.

THE IOWA STATE HYBRID CORN STUDIES

What has loosely been referred to here as the hybrid corn studies is actually a series that went well beyond the diffusion of hybrid corn. The first of these studies to be published is by Ryan and Gross (1943) and is probably the best known. Some of the studies that followed are Ryan (1948), Gross (1949), and Gross and Taves (1952).

Rogers (1983:34) credits the Ryan and Gross (1943) study with forming what came to be known as the classical diffusion paradigm. I suspect that Rogers' own 1962 volume on diffusion and its successors had more to do with shaping diffusion research than the Ryan and Gross study but Rogers' point is not without merit. Together, the several studies published by the Iowa State authors went a long way toward mapping out a diffusion research agenda.

What was so remarkable about the 1943 Ryan and Gross study? It dealt with a single innovation, hybrid corn; I have already argued that this gave it stature. The first sentence of their (Ryan and Gross, 1943:15) report states that "the introduction of hybrid seed corn has been the most striking technical advance in midwestern agriculture during the past decade." Over forty years later one could probably justify an even stronger statement.

Beyond their focus on a critical innovation, however, Ryan and Gross helped to set the stage for a communications approach to diffusion research. The authors determined farmers' sources of original knowledge of hybrid corn as well as the source considered most influential. Salespersons were identified as the source of original knowledge by 49 percent of farmer respondents, far more than any other source, and respondents identified neighbors as most influential (45.5 percent), with salespersons in second place (32 percent). The role and effectiveness of various means of communication with farmers became an important theme in much of the later diffusion research and tied in well with the interests reflected in the Hoffer study that I cited earlier.

The Ryan and Gross (1943) study is also noteworthy in that it documented the diffusion of hybrid corn in as least a limited sample of Iowa farmers (N=259, in two communities) as a patterned process over time. The 1943 article included a frequency distribution of farmers' first use of hybrid corn between 1927 and 1941 and an explicit comparison between that observed distribution and the bell-shaped normal distribution. Plotting the observed frequencies on a cumulative basis over time would of course have yielded an S-shaped distribution. Ryan and Gross (1943:21-23) were careful to note that their observed distribution did *not* perfectly conform to the normal curve. They explicitly avoided treatment of the similarity between the observed frequency distribution and the normal curve as other than an "interesting analogy" and called for further inductive research to determine the shape of the diffusion curve. Nevertheless, their data did suggest that diffusion was a patterned process.

Ryan (1948) took a further step in pursuing the question of the shape of the diffusion curve. He used secondary data for the state of Iowa as a whole to determine whether the S-shaped pattern observed in the two-community sample was more than a local phenomenon. The same pattern was indeed observed, and Ryan (1948:276-277) documented some regional variability in the timing of the diffusion process throughout the state.

Ryan (1948:279-293) also followed up another point that had been identified in the earlier study. Statewide data confirmed the earlier findings that farmers first used hybrid seed corn on only a fraction of their corn acreage. After a year or two, trial use was expanded to 100 percent adoption. The general idea of trial before full adoption and the corresponding implications that the farmers' decision-making process extended over a considerable period of time are both ideas that were repeatedly addressed in later research.

Gross (1949) analyzed some additional data from the earlier two-community sample and in doing so helped to map out another set of research issues. The objective in the 1949 analysis was to determine whether farmer characteristics related to adoption of hybrid seed corn (not reported earlier) also serve to predict adoption of a second innovation. That second innovation was in fact a set of practices that were being recommended for eradication of worms and other organisms in hogs. Gross (1949) showed that adopters of the set of hog sanitation practices tended to be better educated than non-adopters, had larger farms and higher farm incomes, and had more contact with farm information sources and organizations. Interestingly, tenure status was not related to adoption, and adopters of the hog sanitation practices tended to be older than non-adopters. More broadly, however, the age variable was the only one showing a reversal in comparing farmer characteristics as predictors of the two innovations. Gross (1949) concluded his analysis by suggesting that there might exist a trait typology – a set of farm operator characteristics – that could be useful in predicting adoption of innovations.

The general idea of a possible typology of farmer characteristics was much more thoroughly analyzed later by Gross and Taves (1952). In that study, still drawing on data from the earlier two-community sample, the authors considered a total of ten innovations. Separate tests were made to determine whether each of twenty-five farm operator characteristics was significantly related to adoption of each of the ten innovations and in a logically consistent manner. In general, Gross and Taves (1952) concluded that it might not be possible to isolate a small battery of farm operator characteristics that would consistently predict adoption behaviors. Not one of the twenty-five characteristics they examined predicted adoption across all ten innovations at a statistically acceptable level (.10)

Gross and Taves (1952) did, however, find that seven farm operator characteristics were consistent predictors of adoption in the sense that the relationships were in the expected direction. Six other characteristics were consistent with respect to sign for nine out of ten innovations. Incidentally, farm size and farm income were among the more consistent predictors. Gross and Taves (1952:324-325) made two inferences based on the results I've described. First, as already mentioned, evidence for a typology of farm operator characteristics that would consistently predict adoption of innovations might be viewed as suggestive but clearly not conclusive. And second, as a hedge against the first inference, Gross and Taves (1952:327) suggested that it might be possible to classify innovations into groupings so as to enhance predictability. They suggested that innovations in fairly wide use were more consistently related to predictors than innovations just coming into use. And they also suggested that adoption of innovations involving a small capital outlay might be more predictable than other adoptions. Both of the ideas concerning characteristics of innovations have figured in later research.

Without adding more detail on the Iowa State studies I will conclude this section by saying that the focus on individual farm operator characteristics, noted about, is probably the single best defining characteristic of the diffusion studies that proliferated in the 1950s and 1960s. The individual's position in the social structure

8

was obviously not ignored, but the search for farm operator characteristics tended to focus on linkages between the individual and various sources of influence and information. A socio-psychological approach, coupled with survey techniques well suited to that approach, has been dominant in diffusion research, and especially so in the early years.

SOME REASONS FOR A TAKE-OFF IN DIFFUSION RESEARCH

As pointed out earlier, research on adoption of agricultural innovations proliferated in the 1950s and later (Christenson and Garkovich, 1985). From the perspective of the 1980s it would be easy to argue that the research was technology driven. Dorner (1983:77) among others reminds us that the "green revolution" in U.S. agriculture is a relatively recent phenomenon. Hybrid corn was first introduced in the late 1920s. Widespread use of commercial fertilizers became evident in the 1950s, and chemical pest control is more recent still.[4] The substantial yield increases that such developments fostered date from the decade of the 1940s or later. Dorner by no means takes a technologically determinist position but it is a fact that U.S. agriculture and that of other industrialized nations has been radically transformed in recent decades (for productivity data on U.S. agriculture over time see Binswanger, 1984:53). Transformation of agriculture in the rest of the world is going on now.

I think that one can argue that a series of technological developments, for example, hybrid corn and the high yielding varieties of wheat and rice, have helped to spark and *maintain* an interest in research on diffusion. I think that the early surge in research, largely in the United States, had more to do with the nature of rural sociology and its organizational context than with technology, however. Earlier I argued that diffusion research represented something of a continuation of research interest in effective communication with farm audiences. This argues for continuity as an underlying factor. While I also argued that hybrid corn, because of its yield improvement potential, attracted attention to diffusion phenomena, I think that the response of rural sociologists had little to do with hybrid corn as such.

One can argue that there was probably a backlog of technology available to farmers in the 1940s and 1950s. Given what is now known about the diffusion process any such backlog is probably always to be found. It would be difficult to argue that the bulk of any backlog of technology awaiting diffusion in the 1940s had anything like the yield improvement potential of hybrid corn, however. And yet studies were mounted to account for the diffusion of pasture improvement practices, green manuring, hog sanitation, and so on.

I think that a major reason for the surge in diffusion research stems from the fact that rural sociologists recognized that such studies would permit them to "join the team." This is not the place to trace out the periodic identity crises that rural sociologists experience (see, for example, Summers, 1983, and the papers that follow in that issue of *The Rural Sociologist*). Suffice it to say that uncertainty about a constituency or clientele group and uncertainty about professional stature are topics that come up with some regularity. In my opinion, diffusion research presented an opportunity to do work in harmony with the production emphasis of colleagues in colleges of agriculture, the obvious client being the farmer. The inference that research administrators might look with favor on such work follows logically (though I have no way of documenting that proposition).

I am arguing that research on diffusion presented an opportunity to do something "worthwhile" in the eyes of agricultural colleagues. That, coupled with a drive to do rigorous empirical work (i.e., respectable work in the eyes of sociological colleagues), the correlated popularity of the sample survey, and the growing dominance of a socio-psychological perspective in the discipline (cf. Lantz, 1984) all contributed to both the increasing popularity of diffusion research and the particular form that it took.

Finally, if I were to be so bold as to suggest that the factors I have listed above might be viewed as necessary conditions for an increasing interest in diffusion, I would also suggest a candidate for the status of sufficient cause. In my opinion, the S-shaped diffusion curve, along with variations in its form, facilitated the definition of research problem statements (and thus obtaining research support and carrying out the work). For example, one of the more common themes pursued in this research area involves the proposition that interpersonal interaction among farmers accounts for the "snowballing" of the diffusion curve, from a slow rate of adoption at first to a much more rapid rate. Variations in the slopes of diffusion curves across different innovations of course attracted attention to the possibility of systematic differences among innovations that could affect their rates of diffusion. The merits of these particular problem areas are not at issue here. My point is that the existence of a patterned process made it relatively easy to state research questions. Another way of saying the same thing is, *ceteris paribus*, it was easier to do research on diffusion than on many other topics (cf. Rogers, 1983:90-91).

NOTES

1. Another aspect of the cultural lag hypothesis worth mentioning here is that the idea of leading and lagging elements in cultural change is of little consequence unless it results in a perception of maladjustment between the elements. Such maladjustment is presumed to be a consequence of differences in change rates. Ogburn dealt extensively with consequences, both negative and positive, but that idea was not quickly picked up by diffusion researchers.

2. Chapin (1928:369-384) noted that abandonment of both of these forms of government *also* followed the same type of pattern over time. The curves referred to above describe net adoption. The "permanency" of adoption has been controversial in the literature of rural sociology, but I'm not aware of any research dealing with abandonment as a patterned process.

3. One can also speculate that the medium of publication, the experiment station bulletin rather than the journal article, contributed to a relative lack of attention to the study.

4. Johnson (1985:145) makes a considerably broader point when he argues that the highly regarded U.S. land grant system was able to do little beyond maintaining itself until about 1900. Any substantial capacity for impacting development came later and was dependent upon a variety of factors beyond the system itself.

First Wave

2

Institutionalization of Diffusion Research

The number of diffusion studies increased quite rapidly after the early 1940s. I regard the number of articles published on that topic in *Rural Sociology* as a reasonable measure of interest among rural sociologists, because diffusion research got its start among subscribers and contributors to that journal. Christenson and Garkovich (1985:512) report that 0.4 percent of all articles in *Rural Sociology* dealt with diffusion in the 1936-45 period. That compares with 4.7 percent of all articles in the 1946-55 period and 7.0 percent in 1956-65. While such percentages obviously leave plenty of room for research reports on other topics, rate of increase in diffusion research reports is impressive.

Until approximately the 1960s most of the rural sociological research on diffusion was concentrated in the United States. The following chapter will deal with the spread of diffusion research to other parts of the world, primarily to the developing countries. In this chapter I will describe the gradual institutionalization of a particular approach to diffusion phenomena. In the course of making that description it should become apparent that diffusion studies were undertaken in many different locations. In spite of the multiplicity of relatively small-scale studies, however, a substantial degree of consensus emerged. I will first describe the main outlines of that consensus approach to diffusion and then describe some of its elements. In later chapters I will discuss criticisms of that consensus approach.

Figure 1
Diffusion as a Linear Phenomenon

Technology	Technology	Utilization
		of Technology
Generation	Transfer	By Farmers

THE CLASSICAL MODEL

Recent critiques of diffusion research make reference to a "classical" approach in the early years. What does that mean? Rogers (1983:333-334) uses the term "classical" to denote an essentially linear approach to diffusion phenomena that characterized many of the early studies. Figure 1 specifies such an approach. Agricultural innovations are assumed to be generated in some centralized manner, implicitly in a public sector institution such as an agricultural experiment station. Improved technology is then transferred to the ultimate user, the farmer, in a presumably organized manner. Both public and private sector organizations may be involved in the transfer process. Given the location of many rural sociologists in colleges of agriculture, however, it is not surprising that extension should have been singled out for primary attention in the transfer process. The farmer as ultimate user of improved technology tends to be treated as subject to change agent stimuli, as a relatively passive recipient of the technology from the perspective of the linear model shown in Figure 1.

One of the major defining characteristics of diffusion research through the 1960s is that it tended to view the process as linear, as a rational, planned change process. I do not disagree with that characterization, though I tend to think of the so-called classical model of diffusion research as taking the form depicted in Figure 2. There the adoption decision of the farmer is the focal point. Implicitly, the farmer is again viewed as passive, responding to various stimuli from extension personnel, the media, farm organizations, and so on.

Figure 2
A Widely Accepted Approach to the Adoption of Agricultural Innovations

The conceptualization shown in Figure 2 is not explicit about the source of agricultural innovations. Another set of variables is drawn into the picture, however. The farmer's act of adoption is viewed as taking place in a certain situation. Size of farm and farm income were typically included in diffusion studies as characteristics of the situation that affected action. Farmer characteristics also were typically taken into account. Tenure status, age or stage of family life cycle, and level of education are representative of the kinds of individual characteristics thought to affect action with respect to innovations.

In Figure 2 I have drawn on the graphic convention of path analysis to specify both direct and indirect influences on farmers' adoption decisions. Path analytic techniques did not come into use among sociologists until diffusion research had declined in popularity. Nevertheless, I think that the rationale for selection and analysis of variables to account for differences in adoption behavior is fairly well represented by Figure 2. As bivariate analytic techniques gradually gave way to multivariate techniques the conceptual model shown in Figure 2 emerged as the consensus view of how adoption behavior could be analyzed. The defining characteristic of that model is that it represents a socio-psychological approach to understanding behavior. Much of the diffusion research of the 1950s and 1960s was concerned with operationally defining the farmer's adoption behavior, with identifying information flows to the farmer, and with characteristics of the individual and his (not her) situation that might affect information flows. It is fair to say that the innovations of interest were assumed to be good for the farmer and for society.

DEFINING ADOPTION

The question whether to treat a farmer's adoption decision as a distinctive act or as part of a more general propensity to act in a certain way attracted much attention from rural sociologists. This question was already addressed in the early Iowa studies described in Chapter 1. In those studies the uniqueness or generality of the adoption decision was addressed by determining whether presumed antecedents of a decision to adopt a given innovation were the same as the antecedents of a second and third such decision. The results were not clear-cut but the stage was set for further studies to determine whether there might exist a farmer trait complex that could serve to predict adoption behavior.

In general, later research took a different approach by asking whether a farmer's adoption of one innovation could serve to predict that farmer's behavior with respect to other innovations. The research question became: Is a propensity to adopt innovations itself a measurable trait? Data shown in tables 1 and 2 can serve to illustrate the approach. These data are taken from some of my own research (Fliegel, 1956) and are quite representative of other results from the same time period.

The data shown in Table 1 were obtained from a sample of 170 farm owner-operators in a single Wisconsin county in 1952. Only respondents who had high-school-age children living at home were included in the sample, thus in general the variability in farmer traits across respondents was reduced. Each respondent was asked whether each of eleven recommended farm practices was being used in the year preceding the survey. These yes/no responses were then intercorrelated with the results as shown in Table 1.

Perhaps the most striking fact illustrated in Table 1 is that the correlations are almost uniformly low. At first glance it would seem that farmers' adoption of one innovation is not a good predictor of adoption of others. Several of the correlations are in fact

Table 1
Matrix of Intercorrelations of Adoption of Eleven Farm Practices

	1	2	3	4	5	6	7	8	9	10	11
1	-	.22	.15	.15	.04	.11	.09	.19	.02	.09	.12
2	-	-	.15	.19	.10	.19	.10	.15	.15	.04	.26
3	-	-	-	.18	.04	.04	.03	.12	.06	.13	.15
4	-	-	-	-	.22	-.04	.07	.45	.22	.15	.13
5	-	-	-	-	-	.01	.06	.08	.25	.18	.08
6	-	-	-	-	-	-	-.07	.00	.07	.12	.08
7	-	-	-	-	-	-	-	.09	.07	.07	.14
8	-	-	-	-	-	-	-	-	.02	-.02	-.01
9	-	-	-	-	-	-	-	-	-	.22	.11
10	-	-	-	-	-	-	-	-	-	-	.17
11	-	-	-	-	-	-	-	-	-	-	-

Note: From Fliegel, Frederick C. (1956)

These practices are: (1) use of 200 lbs. or more of recommended fertilizer per acre on pasture with last seeding, (2) soil test within past three years, (3) use at any time of high nitrogen fertilizer on corn as side dressing, (4) use of registered sire in 1951, (5) clipping of cows' udders in 1951, (6) use of hay baler in 1951, (7) use of 2-4-D for weed control in 1951, (8) use of artificial insemination in 1951, (9) use of milking machine in 1951, (10) use of mechanical milk cooler in 1951, (11) use of residual fly spray on barn in 1951.

negative, though near zero. The highest single correlation is only .45, between use of registered sire and use of artificial insemination for dairy cows. Since the use of these two practices is, to a degree, necessarily related, the general picture of low intercorrelations is reinforced.

Nevertheless, undaunted by discouraging results, the intercorrelations show in Table 1 were subjected to a factor analysis (done by hand on a mechanical calculator). Results of the factor analysis are shown in Table 2. Even if one discounts the rather more relaxed standards of the day which permitted acceptance of minimal factor loadings of only 0.2, one can infer from Table 2 that it demonstrates some evidence of a common, adoption dimension.

Table 2

Correlation of Adoption of Eleven Farm Practices with First General Factor

Practices	Correlation With Factor 1
1. Fertilizer	.444
2. Soil Test	.553
3. Side Dressing	.420
4. Registered Sire	.650
5. Clip Udders	.426
6. Baler	.207
7. Weed Control	.275
8. Artificial Insemination	.467
9. Milking Machine	.457
10. Milk Cooler	.417
11. Fly Spray	.456

Note: From Fliegel, Frederick C. (1956).

Though inferences based on Table 2 were stated with considerable caution, the results were presented as evidence that a general propensity to adopt agricultural innovations, albeit a weak tendency, could be said to exist.

Rogers and Rogers (1961) did an analysis of data from six different studies to assess the question of innovativeness as a general dimension, and several other measurement issues, in a systematic manner. They attempted to determine whether general measures of adoption behavior, scales or indexes, were reasonably valid, reliable, internally consistent, and unidimensional. Their general conclusion (Rogers and Rogers, 1961:336) was that "adoption scales are reasonably valid, reliable and internally consistent. Clear cut support of unidimensionality, however, is not apparent." The latter point, concerning unidimensionality, will be discussed later in this chapter. More broadly, their conclusions concerning the validity, reliability, and internal consistency of adoption scales or indexes served to consolidate the tendency among those doing research on diffusion to treat innovativeness as a general dimension. Treatment of innovativeness as essentially a personality trait, in turn, bolstered the general tendency to take a socio-psychological approach to the diffusion process.

Although in general supporting the operational definition of adoption behavior as a personality trait, Rogers and Rogers (1961) also recommended several means of improving measurement of that trait. They recommended that increasing the number of innovations included in an index would serve to improve the measurement qualities of such indexes. They also warned against treating failure to adopt a given innovation which might be simply inapplicable to the farmer's situation as non-adoption.[1] The question of applicability is worth mention here because that theme has recurred in the diffusion literature, most recently under the more general heading of "appropriate technology." And finally Rogers and Rogers (1961) recommended that adoption indexes should take into account time of adoption as well as the sheer fact of adoption. The farmer who adopted an innovation ten years ago is more of an innovator than the farmer who adopted last year, in other words.

However intuitively appealing the inclusion of the time dimension in adoption indexes might be, the pursuit of that measurement direction points up another of the measurement problems that plague the social sciences. Rogers and Rogers (1961:332) assessed farmers' ability to reliably recall date of adoption by comparing responses obtained from the same farmers two years after an initial interview. They concluded that "respondent recall of adoption date was not completely consistent over the two-year period, but it was fairly accurate within usable limits."

Coughenour (1965) took a further step in assessing the reliability of recall data. Coughenour (1965) took data from a small (N=48) sample of farmer respondents concerning date of adoption of four innovations. These respondents had been interviewed in 1957, 1959, and again in 1962. Coughenour (1965:188) concluded that "for no practice did more than 21 percent of the farmers report the same annual dates of adoption on any two surveys." Moreover, his analysis showed that mean differences in reported years since adoption ranged from 2.37 years to 3.61 years across the four innovations. The reported discrepancies in years since adoption were both positive and negative. That is to say reported dates of adoption might be either earlier or later when the same farmer was interviewed a second time. And finally, the data showed that the discrepancies in reported dates of adoption tended to increase with the passage of time.

Coughenour (1965) did not conclude that recall data should not be used in constructing adoption indexes. Instead he recommended that improvements in interviewing techniques, among other things, could serve to reduce measurement error. To the dispassionate observer, results such as those reported by Coughenour (1965) might well serve to discourage further work on diffusion phenomena. The results are presented here as a reminder that robust measures are in short supply in the social sciences (Stokes and Miller, 1985:553-555). With specific reference to diffusion research, the reliance on recall data has been troublesome not only for assessing time of adoption, but for assessing information flows. Specifying the "first" source of information about an innovation or the "most influential" source, is of course, heavily dependent on the respondents' ability to recall events in the past.

DEFINING ANTECEDENTS OF ADOPTION

A general sketch of the expected antecedents of adoption of farm innovations has already been presented in Figure 2. As indicated, the theoretical rationale for selecting antecedents for study was relatively straightforward. The farmer was viewed as an actor in a given situation. Situational characteristics were viewed as constraining the farmer's decision to adopt or not adopt an innovation. Personal characteristics similarly were viewed as constraints on action. Given the constraints, the farmer's action was viewed as influenced by information flows concerning innovations and somewhat less directly by linkages with the large society that were presumed to influence information flows and, to a degree, influence attitudes toward technological change. A major idea underlying the rationale just described is that the farmer's adoption decision was regarded as a voluntary act.

Gradual acceptance of the idea that a farmer's decision to adopt an innovation could be treated at a more general level, as a general propensity to adopt that might be called innovativeness, blended well with a quest for combinations or clusters of factors

Institutionalization

presumed to influence that propensity to act in a certain way. The gradual shift from bivariate to multivariate analytic techniques in the 1950s and 1960s also fostered the quest for such combinations of factors. It is convenient to describe such combinations of factors in terms of the graphics widely used in diffusion research. Figure 3, below, which capitalizes on the resemblance of the diffusion curve to the normal curve, represents one of those graphic conventions.

I have chosen to borrow Figure 3 from a publication by the North Central Rural Sociology Committee (1961) in order to make several points. First, the publication represented a regional effort to coordinate research and consolidate findings about diffusion. Research on diffusion gained popularity, as indicated earlier, and that popularity gave rise to coordinative efforts. Second, the publication in question was an extension circular. The latter fact illustrates

Figure 3
Distribution of Farmers Among Five Categories According to Time of Adoption

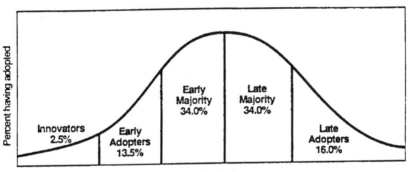

Note: Adapted from North Central Rural Sociology Committee, Subcommittee for the Study of Diffusion of Farm Practices, *Adopters of New Farm Ideas: Characteristics and Communications Behavior*. North Central Regional Extension Publication, No. 13. East Lansing, Michigan: Michigan State University, Cooperative Extension Service, 1961.

interest in disseminating information about diffusion to audiences other than just those doing the research. Third, it is not accidental that the publication stemmed from an effort in the North Central Region of the United States, for much of the early research was concentrated in that region. Fourth, and finally, the substantive importance of Figure 3 is that it is based on the normal curve and

21

utilizes two parameters of that distribution, the mean and the standard deviation.

Figure 3 describes a categorization of farmers with respect to time of adoption in terms of average time elapsed between first introduction and 100 percent adoption of innovations in a given population. Those farmers more than two standard deviations earlier in time of adoption than the average were labeled innovators. Similarly, those farmers between one and two standard deviation earlier in time of adoption than the average farmer were classified as early adopters. Then, farmers within one standard deviation, earlier or later, were labeled early and late majority respectively. And finally, those farmers more than one standard deviation later than the average farmer in adoption are labeled late adopters in the figure. There is no inherent reason for dividing the distribution shown in Figure 3 into 5 rather than six categories. Six categories could have provided symmetry by subdividing late adopters, also called laggards in the same publication, into the late and extremely late, for example. It proved to be empirically difficult to identify farmer traits that corresponded to extreme lateness of adoption, however, and the five categories shown in the figure came to be accepted as standard categories in the diffusion literature.

The North Central Rural Sociology Committee (1961) publication from which Figure 3 was taken treated the diffusion curve as identical to the normal distribution. Publication as an extension circular would tend to preclude discussion of technical details concerning degree of correspondence between the two curves. Rogers (1958) had provided a fairly sound basis for claiming correspondence, however. Rogers (1958) noted, among other things, that Ryan and Gross (1943) had determined that the diffusion of hybrid corn in their Iowa sample only approximated the normal distribution. Rogers (1958) analyzed data from several different data sets to determine, in a more systematic manner, whether the patterns of diffusion of single innovations conformed to the normal distribution. In total, he conducted six such tests, in each case using a goodness of fit test to determine whether the observed distribution conformed to normality. Three tests confirmed the hypothesis of normality and three did not. Rogers (1958:353) also tested the same proposition with an index of adoption behavior based on twenty-five farm practices, the observed distribution in that case conforming to normality. Rogers (1958:354) was suitably cautious in drawing conclusions, stating that diffusion curves were found to "approach normality." It is fair to say, however, that many later studies took it for granted that innovativeness was a normally distributed human trait, and thus the categories shown in Figure 3 came to be accepted as not only useful but reflective of reality.

Table 3, also taken from the regional publication, represents a summary of at least some of the antecedents of farmer adoption by adopter category. I will not attempt to describe the studies that provided the basis for this summary of farmer characteristics. One must recognize, on the one hand, that any such summary cannot depict the varying degrees of certainty behind the brief description of supposedly different types of farmers. And, on the other hand, one must also recognize that it is tempting to treat tentative typologies as accurate descriptions of reality. It is my opinion that the laggard category (see Table 3), in particular, made it rather easy to do what later came to be called "blaming the victim." That is to say, if diffusion is viewed as the planned transfer of desirable technology to farmers, then it is tempting to view those who are late in adoption or never adopt as superstitious, uneducated, parochial, and generally rather loutish characters. In recent years, as the appropriateness of some farm innovations came to be questioned, and as questions about adoption as an act of will came to be raised, the entire socio-psychological approach to diffusion phenomena came to be questioned. Had the typologies of farmer characteristics been treated as heuristic devices rather than concrete entities some later criticisms might have been avoided.

In general, the types of farmer and situational characteristics listed at the left in Table 3 are a reasonable representation of the variables included in research designs by various authors. The descriptive terms in the cells of the table, for example with respect to education, reflect the findings from research to that point in time, largely from the United States. Later efforts to apply the approach illustrated to research in developing countries made it necessary to reformulate operational definitions of many variables and thus also descriptive statements about findings. In a setting in which most of a farm population is not literate, and where printed sources of farm information are not available even if farmers could read, details of the type of approach illustrated in the table had to be modified

Institutionalization

Table 3
Summary of Characteristics and Communication Behavior of Adopter Categories

Characteristic or Behavior	Innovators	Early Adopters	Majority		Laggards or Late Adopters
			Early	Late	
1. Time of adoption	First 2.5% to adopt new ideas	Next 13.5% to adopt	Next 34% to adopt	Next 34% to adopt	Last 16% to adopt
2. Attitudes & values	Scientific and Venturesome	Progressive	More conservative & traditional	Skeptical of new ideas	Ag. Magic and folk beliefs; fear of debt
3. Abilities	High level of education; ability to deal with abstractions	Above average education	Slightly above average education	Slightly below average education	Low level of education; have difficulty dealing with abstractions & relationships
4. Group memberships	Leaders in county wide or state organizations; travel widely	Leaders in organizations within the community	Many informal contact within the community	Little travel out of community; little activity in formal organizations	Few membership in formal organizations other than church; semi-isolates
5. Social status	Highest social status, but their farming practice may not be accepted	High social status; looked to by neighbors as "good farmer"	About average social status	About average social status	Lowest social status
6. Farm businesses	Largest, most specialized, and most efficient	Large farms; slightly less specialized & efficient	Slightly larger than average sized farms	Slightly smaller than average sized farms	Small farms, low incomes; seldom farm owners
7. Sources of information	Scientists; other innovators; research bulletins	Highest contact with local change agents; farm magazines; extension bulletin	Farm magazines; friends & neighbors	Friends and neighbors	Mainly friends & neighbors; radio farm shows

Note: From North Central Rural Committee (1961).

DEFINING THE PROCESS OF ADOPTION

Reference was made earlier to the general idea that an innovation might be tried out on a small scale prior to full adoption. Ryan and Gross (1943) had noted this fact and set the stage for conceptualizing adoption decision-making as a process extending over a period of time. It is the communications aspect of this general idea that attracted most attention in diffusion research. That is to say, effective information and knowledge transfer were long-standing concerns, and the possibility that a given communications medium might be more or less effective at different points in a decision-making process extending over time became attractive as a focus for research.

A study carried out by Copp, Sill, and Brown (1958)[2] can serve to illustrate the communications approach to the adoption process. These authors drew on several earlier studies that had conceptualized the adoption process as consisting of a series of stages from first becoming aware of an innovation to ultimately adopting that innovation for use on the particular respondent's farm. Copp, Sill, and Brown (1958) based their work on the proposition that it made sense to view adoption decisions as involving a process over time, but that the precise number of stages employed to conceptualize that process was arbitrary. In other words, they argued that debate over whether there were "really" three stages in the process, or five stages, was not productive. They took the position that the criterion by which to judge a given conceptualization should be its utility in gaining insight into the process. In addition, they were aware that putting questions to farmers about their sources of information in terms of assumed stages might well bias farmers' responses to conform to the question format. In order to avoid that potential bias they used open-ended questions and indirect cues to get respondents to reconstruct their information seeking behavior with respect to three different innovations.

Copp, Sill, and Brown (1958) obtained individual reconstructions of information seeking behavior from 175 dairy farmers in a single Pennsylvania county. The three innovations involved in the study were all relevant to dairy farming. They then analyzed the individual case histories and determined that it was possible to classify farmers' experiences into five categories or stages, as follows:

25

1. *Awareness:* The farmer hears of the innovation.
2. *Interest:* The farmer feels the innovation is a workable solution to *a* farm problem.
3. *Acceptance:* The farmer feels the innovation would be useful on *his* farm.
4. *Trial:* The farmer tries the innovation on his farm.
5. *Adoption:* The farmer continues using the innovation.

The tentative definitions of stages that Copp, Sill, and Brown (1958) derived from their data were similar to some of the conceptualizations used in earlier studies and are similar to the definitions of stages that became part of the institutionalized approach to diffusion research. Having tabulated the information sources cited by farmer respondents at various stages in the adoption process, the authors then conducted a test of their conceptual model. At issue were such questions as: Are there patterns in information seeking behavior at different stages in the process? And, if there are patterns, does conformity to the pattern make a difference in respondents' adoption behavior?

Table 4 summarizes the results of the test of the Copp, Sill, and Brown (1958) model. The frequencies shown in the table represent a condensation of individual responses concerning information sources in two categories, the most frequently cited type of source and all other citations. It is apparent that farm magazines and publications provided by the Cooperative Extension Service were the most frequently cited sources of information at the awareness stage, for example. In contrast, face-to-face interaction was the most frequently cited means of obtaining information at the acceptance stage. The authors also devised what are called "progress scores" in the table. Each respondent was given a score ranging from one to five corresponding to the stage in the adoption process that respondent had achieved at the time of the interview. If the respondent had adopted innovation "A," for example, the score would be five, corresponding to the fifth and final stage. If the respondent was aware of and expressed interest in the innovation the score would be two, and so on.

The test of the stage model reported in Table 4 then involved posing the hypothesis that conformity to the dominant pattern of

Table 4
Comparison of Mean Progress Scores for Expected and Other Sources of Farm Information for Four Stages in the Adoption of Three Recommended Farm Practices

Stage	Source	N	A $\bar{X}$ Progress Scores	N	B $\bar{X}$ Progress Scores	N	Innovation C $\bar{X}$ Progress Scores
I.	Awareness						
	Magazines & printed extension	137	3.34	105	3.55	127	1.74
	Other	35	2.49	64	3.27	43	1.40
	Difference in expected direction		yes		yes		yes
II.	Interest						
	Printed & oral extension	50	4.52	41	4.73	17	3.65
	Other	53	3.64	49	3.92	22	3.27
	Difference in expected direction		yes		yes		yes
III.	Acceptance						
	Oral extension & peer influence	44	4.89	30	4.83	8	5.00
	Other	13	4.54	11	5.00	8	4.63
	Difference in expected direction		yes		no		yes
IV.	Trial						
	Printed instructions and/or demonstration	66	4.97	66	4.89	14	4.93
	Other	6	5.00	11	4.91	3	5.00

Note: Adapted from Copp, Sill, and Brown (1958).

obtaining information at each stage of the process should be conducive to achieving a higher level of progress in the adoption process. To put it as a question, does citation of one type of source, a quantitatively preferred source, make a positive difference in progression through the stages to ultimate adoption? The authors concluded that in eight of the nine possible comparisons their expectations were supported.

Two inferences concerning communications strategy are at least partially supported by the data shown in Table 4. First, the mass media are useful in providing first information about an innovation. And second, the mass media are less useful in later stages of decision-making and are replaced as useful information sources by face-to-face contact, especially with expert information sources. Inferences along these lines were incorporated into what I am calling the institutionalized approach to diffusion which prevailed prior to about 1970. Of greater consequence is the fact that such inferences have been incorporated into communications strategies designed to implement change.

DEFINING ATTRIBUTES OF INNOVATIONS

Particular attributes of innovations began to receive attention with the initiation of research on diffusion in agriculture. Ryan and Gross (1943) had cited hybrid corn's massive potential for increased yield and raised questions about generalizing from the hybrid corn research results to other innovations. The dominant tendency in diffusion research clearly developed in the direction of treating all farm innovations as equivalent with an emphasis on working toward better measures of farmers' presumed general propensity to adopt improved technology. Nevertheless, the kinds of measurement problems that I discussed earlier in this chapter continued to stimulate some interest in differentiating among innovations in terms of types or particular characteristics. In either case, the research focus remained on individual farmers' decision-making behavior with respect to technology assumed to be beneficial to them.

Barnett (1953), writing from a general socio-cultural change perspective in the 1950s, gave a special boost to diffusion research in two ways. First, he took a position on the debate as to whether diffusion was worth serious attention as a stimulus to social and cultural change by treating innovation (or invention) and diffusion as twin processes, in some respects inseparable from each other. And second, he dealt at some length with particular attributes of innovations that he felt were implicated in the diffusion process. Among these were

Figure 4
Cumulative Percentages of Farmers Adopting Two Improved Practices Over a Seventeen-Year Period, Susquehanna County, Pennsylvania

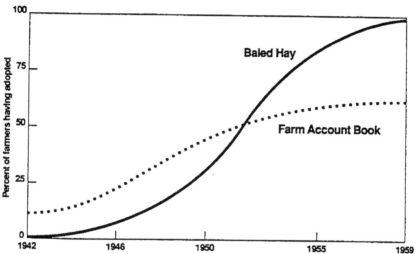

Note: From *Differences among improved farm practices as related to rates of adoption* (Bulletin 691) by F. C. Fliegel and J. E. Kivlin, 1962a, University Park, Penn.: Agricultural Experiment Station, Pennsylvania State University.

compatibility between old and new, efficiency, cost, and the advantage associated with the new, including prestige gains.

The key idea in studies of attributes of innovations is the simple notion that innovations are not all alike, and that some of the differences may be influential in the diffusion process. Figure 4, taken from a study of Pennsylvania dairy farmers (Fliegel and Kivlin, 1962a), can serve as an illustration. The S curve of diffusion research is at least vaguely recognizable in the figure. Both of the innovations were considered to be critical-to dairying. Record keeping, a financial practice, illustrates well the importance of capital management in an increasingly capital intensive agriculture. And the practice of baling hay involves use of a machine to compress harvested and cured hay into compact bales for ease in handling. The hay baler replaced a range of considerably more labor-intensive and physically demanding techniques for removal of hay from the field to a storage site and eventual distribution to animals as feed.

The immediate point to be made with respect to the curves shown in Figure 4 is that the rates at which the two innovations were accepted by sample farmers are quite different. One innovation had been adopted relatively quickly by virtually all farmers in the study area by 1959, the other much more slowly. The question then is: Are there particular attributes of those innovations and others like them that can help to explain why the adoption rates differ?

Research on attributes of innovations can easily become complex in that it is desirable to include a relatively large number of innovations and to assess those innovations with respect to a number of attributes. The study from which Figure 4 is taken began with an exhaustive list of fifty-nine innovations, all judged to be relevant to a sample of 229 commercial dairy farmers.[3] A list of possible attributes of innovations was then drawn up, as illustrated in Table 5. It should be obvious that obtaining ratings for 11 attributes, as shown in Table 5, across fifty-nine innovations requires a total of 11 x 59 = 649 individual judgements. While that is by no means an impossible task it puts a decided strain on the respondent. The usual survey techniques are not well suited for long series of questions involving detailed judgements. Perhaps for that reason alone inquires into the relationship between attributes of innovations and rate of adoption never became popular.

In order to minimize the data gathering difficulties referred to above, the rating scale shown in Table 5 were presented to a panel of twenty "expert" judges from the study area. These judges were assembled and were asked to rate the innovations, using a paper-and-pencil format, from the perspective of the typical farmer in the sample.[4] The list of attributes shown in Table 5 is heavily weighted toward the general question of "relative advantage." That is, it was assumed that an innovation better than what it is intended to replace, advantageous to the adopter relative to the old way of doing things, will be adopted relatively quickly.

Institutionalization

Table 5
An Example of Rating Scales Used in a Study of Farm Innovation Attributes Among Dairy Farmers

		1	2	3	4	
1.	Low initial cost	1	2	3	4	High initial cost
2.	Little or no continuing cost	1	2	3	4	Fairly large continuing costs
3.	Cost quickly recovered	1	2	3	4	Cost recovered slowly
4.	Easily tried on a small scale	1	2	3	4	Not divisible for trial
5.	Much mechanical attraction	1	2	3	4	Little or no mechanical attraction
6.	Simple to use or understand	1	2	3	4	Somewhat difficult to use or understand
7.	Little or no disagreement with past experience	1	2	3	4	Fairly large disagreement with past experience
8.	Always associated with dairying – a dairy practice	1	2	3	4	No necessary association with dairying—not a dairy practice
9.	Saves much time in getting immediate job done	1	2	3	4	No saving, or saving of time not involved
10.	Much saving of physical discomfort	1	2	3	4	No saving, or physical discomfort not involved
11.	Much financial or other advantage to over-all farm program.	1	2	3	4	Little or no advantage – just an economically sound practice.

Note: From Fliegel and Kivlin (1962a)

Institutionalization

Defining "advantage" in practical terms is not a simple matter. Financial advantage is emphasized in the list shown in Table 5. The illustrative list of attributes breaks the concept of advantage down into a series of items having to do with costs and returns and also attempts to capture the totality in the final item listed – overall advantage. The presumed components of advantage treat costs – both initial as well as continuing costs – and also rate of return. In each case the assumption was made that lower costs and more rapidly recovered costs are preferred by the adopter. In addition, it was assumed that advantage may include reduced labor costs (item 9), and the closely associated notion of a reduction in demand for labor to do unpleasant tasks (item 10).

Another attribute that received considerable attention in diffusion studies is the general notion of divisibility for trial. The possibility of trying an innovation on a small scale before full adoption can be viewed as a risk reduction measure and therefore part of the financial advantage complex discussed above. More commonly, however, divisibility for trial has been viewed from a learning perspective. It is assumed that an individual who has some interest in adoption will be encouraged to do so if first-hand experience can be gained (at a minimal cost) and that experience can then be utilized in full-scale adoption. A direct analog in the introduction of innovations for mass consumption is the practice of distributing free samples for trial.

Finally, appeal to the potential adopter from a learning perspective is also emphasized in two other attributes listed in Table 5. It was assumed that an innovation that is relatively simple, easy to understand and use, would be adopted more readily than one that is complex. It was also assumed that an innovation that fits easily into the context in which it is to be used will be preferred over one that is not compatible with other elements in the larger context.[5] As Barnett (1953) pointed out from a theoretical perspective, the concept of compatibility between innovation and context involves an element of contradiction. Simply put, an innovation that fits smoothly and easily into a context should require minimal learning on the part of the adopter and should therefore diffuse rapidly. On the other hand, an innovation that is minimally disruptive might also be perceived as unattractive if the adopter's objective is precisely to bring about change.

Institutionalization
Table 6 displays results that only partially support the expected relationships between the attribute ratings of innovations and sample farmers' actual adoption behavior. These results deal with the expected relationship only at the simple, bivariate level, but

Table 6
Summary of Expected and Actual Relationships Between Attributes of Farm Practices and Rate of Adoption

Attribute	Correlation Between Attributes and Adoption Rate	
	Expected	Actual
Initial Cost	-	+ .13
Continuing cost	-	+ .18
Rate of recovering cost	+	- .08
Divisibility for trial	+	- .04
Mechanical attraction	+	+ .11
Complexity	-	- .30*
Compatibility	+	+ .28*
Association with dairying	+	- .06
Saving of time	+	+ .41*
Saving of discomfort	+	+ .21
Advantage	+	+ .40*

Note: From Fliegel and Kivlin (1962 b).

can serve to demonstrate that apparently plausible assumptions don't always hold up well when subjected to analysis.

One can conclude from Table 6 that those innovations perceived to provide some overall advantage to the adopter were adopted relatively quickly. Assumptions were made about the components of any such advantage, however, and these assumptions were not supported in several instances. It was assumed that the diary farmers in the study sample would tend to adopt quickly those innovations perceived to involve least capital investment and relatively rapid return on any capital invested. This did not prove to be the case. On the contrary, the sample of full-time, commercial dairy farmers tended to favor innovations involving larger and longer term investments. A later, comparative study (Fliegel et al., 1968) demonstrated that more marginal dairy farmers, with considerably smaller farm operations, tended to act in the short-run "economizing" manner that had been assumed to hold for all.

From Table 6 one can infer that complex innovations were adopted more slowly, as expected, but that the possibility of trying out an innovation on a small scale prior to full adoption was not important. Further, one can conclude that potential labor savings were conducive to more rapid diffusion. The latter inference is at least consistent with the findings regarding cost. An apparent preference for increased capital intensity is not independent of adopting labor-saving innovations, especially machines.

Without dwelling further on the results reported in Table 6, I will state here that inferences discussed above were not necessarily supported by later research. My purpose here has been to illustrate the pursuit of a particular idea within the larger context of diffusion research in agriculture. Some related approaches to the same general idea also deserve mention. Wilkening et al. (1962), for example, proposed a typology that grouped innovations primarily concerned with resource maintenance, on the one hand, as against profit maximization on the other. The general idea has been picked up again recently in connection with research on the diffusion of soil and water conservation practices. In the same study Wilkening et al. (1962:152) also explored the possibility of a four-fold functional typology (e.g., disease control, pasture improvement, and other "end use" categories).

In an earlier study, Wilkening (1950) had proposed that recently introduced innovations might be treated separately, in contrast to innovations already in fairly general use. The objective of the proposed typologies was to improve measurement of adoption behavior by classifying entire innovations on the basis of some dominant characteristic, and then to construct more focused indexes of adoption behavior. That approach, via typologies, as well as the approach via focus on a range of attributes of each innovation, had some impact on diffusion research, but by and large this type of analysis was not systematically incorporated into the mainstream of research on diffusion phenomena.

SOME OTHER ASPECTS OF DIFFUSION RESEARCH

If, as I argued above, the emphasis on attributes of an innovation or types of innovations remained somewhat peripheral to the mainstream of activity, there are many other areas of inquiry that did not become part of the "classic" model either. Several of those will be briefly described here, though at the risk of leaving out others of equal importance.

One early thrust of diffusion research served to temper the dominant tendency to focus on the decision-making behavior of male farm operators. In the context of the agriculture of the American Midwest and of the industrialized societies more generally, it is at least arguable that singling out the farm operator as primary decision-maker would legitimately lead to a focus on males. One of Wilkening's main contributions to diffusion research, however, was to draw attention to the familial context in which such decisions were probably made. One of the themes pursued was to determine whether agreement on goals and aspirations between husband and wife, as well as the level of such goals and aspirations, had an influence on farm practice adoption (Wilkening and Guerrero, 1969). In general the data showed that if both husband and wife had high aspirations (for the farm), then adoption of farm innovations would tend to be favored. Another theme Wilkening pursued was to analyze the implications of involvement by both marital partners in farm tasks and in farm decision-making (see, for example, Wilkening, 1953; Wilkening and Bharadwaj, 1968). Though this line of research went well beyond an exclusive focus on adoption of farm innovations, it helped to broaden the perspective from which farm decision-making was viewed.

Another theme pursued by some of the early diffusion studies was to determine whether the norms and values prevailing in particular localities could help to explain differences in rates of adoption. Hoffer's (1942) study of farmers of Dutch descent, described in the preceding chapter, is one such example. Hoffer addressed the general question as to whether retention of the Dutch cultural heritage might be a factor in accepting technological change. Pedersen (1951) is another relatively early example of this line of inquiry. Pederson (1951) compared Midwestern American samples of farmers of Danish and Polish descent, and concluded that the Danish cultural heritage might favor acceptance of improved technology. Marsh and Coleman's (1954) research on neighborhood norms took a somewhat different approach. A sample of farmers from a single county, fairly homogeneous in ethnic background, was categorized by neighborhood of residence. One objective of the research was then to determine whether neighborhood norms regarding acceptance of farm innovations influenced individual adoption decisions. Though this study lacked independent measures of individual adoption and neighborhood norms, the latter defined as average adoption levels for the neighborhood, the general idea that locality group differences could influence individual decisions has merit and has attracted a moderate amount of research attention over the years. Recent research (e.g., Ashby, 1982) has in a sense redefined the locality group perspective to focus on area differences in agroclimatic conditions.

Finally, rural sociologists also utilized the diffusion approach to analyze adoption of innovations in areas other than agriculture. Rogers' (1983) extensive review of research on diffusion of many different kinds of innovations obviates the need to treat that theme broadly here. I wish only to point out that some of the studies done by rural sociologists dealt with both farm and other innovations simultaneously. Duncan and Kreitlow (1954), for example, set out to determine whether neighborhoods that were homogeneous in terms of residents' ethnic and religious backgrounds would be more receptive to both farm and school innovations than neighborhoods that were heterogeneous. By and large they concluded that neighborhood heterogeneity was conducive to acceptance of change in both spheres of activity. Some of Wilkening's research also dealt with innovations in several areas of activity. For example, the Wilkening (1953) study, cited previously with respect to family decision-making, dealt with acceptance of farming, home, and health practices from that same perspective. In general, however, rural sociologists were only marginally involved in applying the diffusion research perspective outside agriculture (Rogers, 1983).

CONCLUSIONS

In this chapter I have described a proliferation of rural sociological research on diffusion of farm innovations which gradually evolved into a fairly stereotypical approach to diffusion phenomena. I argued that the primary characteristics of the approach were a focus on the individual as decision maker, an emphasis on individual and situational characteristics as potential constraints on decision making, and an emphasis on information transfer as a (and perhaps *the*) means of stimulating change.

In order to account for the institutionalization of the approach to diffusion research I cited several factors. I argued that the fact that diffusion is patterned, with a frequency distribution of individual adoption over time more or less conforming to the normal curve, was conducive to raising certain kinds of research questions. The dominance of a socio-psychological perspective in the discipline as a whole as well as the preference for survey techniques probably influenced the directions taken. And I also argued that rural sociologists may have seen in diffusion research a means of relating more closely to the agricultural production interests of colleagues in colleges of agriculture.

The Ryan and Gross (1943) study and closely related publications by the same authors very probably served as a model for some of the later research. In concluding this chapter I want to highlight some other models or sets of guidelines, however. Diffusion research may well be unique as an area of research in rural sociology in that it attracted a whole series of efforts to collate findings and designate problem areas for further research.

I cited some material from the North Central Rural Sociology Committee (1961) in this chapter. That publication reported a stock-taking and direction-setting effort intended to maximize research productivity and utility. The North Central Rural Sociology Committee (1955) had produced an even earlier publication on the same theme, a publication oriented to a lay audience as well as research specialists. The latter publication was accompanied by a bibliography (North Central Rural Sociology Committee, 1956) originally prepared by Herbert Lionberger. Later, Lionberger (1960) published a much more detailed and annotated bibliography on diffusion research. Lionberger also included summaries of research findings in addition to the annotations. The bibliographic effort alone made it a relatively simple task to take stock of what had been done, and by the same token probably also influenced the direction of later studies.

Institutionalization

Beal and Bohlen's (1957) popular publication on the diffusion process must also be mentioned here. That publication was intended for wide dissemination to change agents, administrators, and the agricultural industry in general. These authors also traveled extensively to present illustrated lectures to a variety of audiences, basically stressing the ideas contained in their 1957 publication.

Last but by no means least I want to stress that Rogers' (1962) book on diffusion and its later successors probably influenced the direction taken by diffusion research more than any other single factor. Rogers was of course involved with and drew upon the kinds of integrative efforts I have cited above. Rogers' book-length treatment, however, included much more detail than shorter publications could possibly handle. Rogers consistently worked toward summarizing diverse findings and stating generalizations on the basis of those findings. The net effect was to thoroughly document what had been done and what, at least in the author's view, remained to be done. The fact that the several editions of Rogers' book were widely distributed, well beyond the confines of rural sociology, and came to be used as teaching texts, has to be viewed as a major factor in institutionalizing the mode of doing diffusion research described in this chapter.

NOTES

1. The data reported in Tables 1 and 2 took applicability of the innovation into account.

2. This article appeared in the June 1958 issue of *Rural Sociology*, an issue devoted entirely to papers on diffusion. That fact in itself is evidence of the salience of diffusion research at the time.

3. The sample was designed to restrict variability in age and education of the farm operator, size of farm operation, and several other characteristics in order to permit the analysis to focus on differences among innovations rather than differences among farmers that were known to affect adoption behavior.

4. A later study (Fliegel and Kivlin, 1966) showed that the panel's ratings differed sufficiently from those of farmers making the adoption decisions to warrant a change of procedures. In practical terms that meant using individual interview techniques with farmer respondents and a substantial reduction in the number of innovations under consideration.

5. Here again, one can note some common ground with the later concern about "appropriate technology."

3

Diffusion Research in the Third World

International events following World War II probably had more to do with the spread of diffusion research to various parts of the globe than did the emergence of new agricultural technologies, until about 1970. In recent years the symbolism of the "green revolution" has focused attention on the implications of radically more productive technology, but in the decades immediately following World War II even moderate increases in food production by whatever means were given a high priority.

India's achievement of independence in 1947 can serve as an example of the global transition from a world system of colonial empires to a system of politically independent but often economically weak nations. The struggle for political independence had inevitably involved the prospect of a better life for masses of people. Like many newly independent nations the bulk of India's labor force had been (and remains) involved in food production, yet supplies were less than ample. Scholars were concerned, not with a green revolution, but with a revolution of rising expectations, and food production was central to that concern.

Generic concerns with the adequacy of food supplies following World War II were underscored by increased awareness of population growth rates. Here one must note that public health measures, such as the use of DDT to control malaria-bearing mosquito populations, had a major impact on death rates while birth rates remained high.[1] Already high rates of population increase rose higher still in many developing nations, and gradually attention shifted from industrial development strategies to an increased commitment to growth in agricultural production.

As the industrialized nations emerged from the repair of the devastating effects of World War II they entered into a period of extended growth. With that growth came a concern about markets and also a concern about the development prospects of third world nations, both former colonies and others as well. With respect to agriculture the first impulse was to directly transfer some of the technologies that had proven effective in increasing food production in the industrialized nations. This did not necessarily mean the transfer of radically more productive technology, however. The Asian countries, and many others, looked to rice and wheat as their staple food crops. Hybrid corn, principally used as animal feed, was not a priority item for such nations, and that remains the case today. The immediate task, then, was to gain wider acceptance of improved cultural practices, better plant materials, and improved plant nutrition including chemical fertilizers. And that type of task, in turn, called for increased efficiency in whatever mechanisms were in place for technology transfer.

To some extent the communications approach to diffusion of agricultural innovations that I described in the last chapter was directly transferred to third world settings via involvement of U.S. universities in an array of development schemes. That doesn't tell the whole story by any means but it is the case that the communications approach was applied. In some cases it was found suitable for providing detailed information to help in planning transfer programs. In other cases it was found wanting and was the occasion for rethinking some aspects of the approach as a whole. It is particularly the latter type of issue that I want to pursue here. Rather than a comprehensive review, I want to present selected studies from the fuller body of diffusion research to demonstrate how diffusion research was applied to third world settings and what lessons came to be learned as a consequence. The communications approach to information transfer – media availability, educational levels, and literacy – made many assumptions about third world settings and about the structural inequalities existing before and resulting from adoption of processes.

COMMUNICATIONS VARIABLES

In retrospect it is perhaps somewhat surprising that questions about the use of mass media as farm information sources should have been put to smallholder farmers in third world settings in the 1960s. We know a great deal more about third world agriculture today than we did a generation ago. Also, a generation ago mass media exposure was assumed to have a more substantial transformative effect on people than is thought to be the case today. There is a whole literature on this topic that I do not address here. In any case, it soon became apparent that information flows in, say, Colombia were not the same as in the midwestern United States.

I cited Colombia as an example of a third world setting above in part because Rogers and Meynen (1965) did a detailed analysis of the Colombian farmers' use of information sources by stage in the adoption process. The Colombian data were compared with results from earlier diffusion studies in the United States.

Rogers and Meynen (1965) obtained data from a sample of 158 Colombian smallholder farmers. Their average farm size was 6.6 acres and they produced a variety of crops. At the time of the interview, in 1963, 65 percent of the sample had adopted a chemical form of weed control (2, 4-D) for use on their farms. Questions were put to these farmers about their use of information sources from first knowledge, or awareness, of the weed spray through trial use of the spray. The authors' purpose was to determine to what extent the pattern of information source usage of the Colombian sample was like the pattern of farmers in the United States.

The biggest single difference in information flows that Rogers and Meynen (1965) documented was that the mass media, most frequently cited by U.S. farmers as a first source of information, were not mentioned by Colombian farmers at all, either as a source of first knowledge or at any other stage. Now, the Colombian respondents did have access to the mass media. Sixty percent of the sample reported daily radio listening and an equal proportion reported reading a newspaper at least once weekly. While the authors did not pursue the question of whether the locally available media actually carried any significant amount of information about farm technology, they reported that the mass media were not useful as information sources for their Colombian sample.

Rogers and Meynen (1965) also tested several propositions about the role of face-to-face communications about farm technology in the Colombian setting. They pursued the general idea of linkages with information sources in the larger society by testing whether "personal-cosmopolite" information sources (extension agents and farm-supply store personnel) were more frequently cited at early stages in the adoption process. That did not prove to be the case for their sample. The Colombian respondents most frequently mentioned "localite" information sources (especially friends and neighbors) for the early stages of the adoption process, including the awareness stage. The personal-cosmopolite sources were preferred at the trial stage, however, where it became important to have detailed information about the quantity to be used, time of application, and so on. Although printed instructions were not mentioned at the trial stage, the reliance on other than local information sources conformed to the U.S. findings.

In summary, what Rogers and Meynen (1965) demonstrated was that literal application of a communications model developed in the industrial north did not work well in a third world setting. One can infer that the mass media were probably not being used to the extent possible. There is no question but that a great deal of effort has gone into preparation of materials for mass media usage in third world settings in recent years.

LITERACY AND INFORMATION TRANSFER

Diffusion research in third world settings confronted questions about the role of literacy that there had been no occasion to confront in earlier studies in the United States. Lionberger (1960), after reviewing the early diffusion studies, took a very cautious stance about the role of farmers' education in the diffusion process. Lionberger (1960:97) stated that:

> The assumption is that schooling facilitates learning, which in turn is presumed to instill a favorable attitude toward the use of improved farm practices. Be that as it may, the relationship between years of schooling and farm practice adoption rates is likely to be indirect, except in cases where persons learn specifically about new practices in school.

In spite of Lionberger's (1960) reasoned and data-based argument, however, the presumption of a positive and direct link between level of education and innovativeness persisted in the diffusion research tradition. In part, the presumption of direct linkage may have stemmed from the conventions of the research tradition itself. The preference for multi-item measures of adoption, and the corresponding practice of categorizing some farmers as "innovators," served to highlight differences in individual characteristics. Innovators were routinely described as relatively high in education and laggards were put at the opposite extreme. As a result it is not surprising that the frequently non-literate farmers in third world settings were more or less automatically assumed to be laggards.

If the typology of adopters lent itself to thinking of the types as concretely reflecting reality, the presumption of a direct link between education and adoption was also bolstered by then current thinking about the development process in general. In the preceding section I made brief reference to an assumption that the mass media could have a transformative effect on traditional (i.e., rural) societies. Lerner's (1958) *The Passing of Traditional Society* was a widely read part of that literature and argued for a strong link between media participation and literacy. In very broad terms Lerner's (1958:57-58) theoretical posture was that urbanization contributed to increasing literacy, the latter contributed to increasing media participation, and the end result was a democratic, participant society. Lerner stressed literacy as transformative and this type of thinking contributed directly to viewing non-literacy as a major deterrent to the introduction of agricultural innovations among farmers in developing countries.

Several detailed analyses of the role of literacy in "traditional" farmers' adoption behavior reported results directly analogous to the conclusion that Lionberger (1960) had reached earlier, that is, that the influence of schooling on farm practice adoption is likely to be indirect. I am assuming here that literacy is a function of schooling and that the differences between measures of literacy, usually treated as a dichotomous variable, and the continuous variable, level of schooling, are not critical in the context of the present discussion.

Bose (1964) reported an analysis of the links between Indian farmers' literacy, their information-seeking behavior, and their adoption of farm innovations. His data showed that both literate and non-literate farmers, if they participated in various village organizations, tended to be high adopters of improved farm technology. He inferred that information about farm innovations could and did flow through face-to-face communication channels. Thus literacy was not necessarily a deterrent to adoption.

A similar study among smallholder farmers in southern Brazil (Fliegel, 1966) reached about the same conclusion. In the study both literacy and level of education (averaging under four years) were analyzed with respect to information source usage and eventual adoption. Aside from differential print media usage, the non-literate and least schooled farmers were about as likely as others to listen to farm radio programs and contact their local extension agents. Information about farm technology was available from a variety of sources, in other words. Thus the least schooled were not necessarily disadvantaged.

In the course of time the tendency to treat convenient analytic categories as concrete reflections of reality has abated. Gusfield's (1967) critique of the tendency to view "tradition" and "modernity" as sharply defined polar opposites was influential in this regard. That critique and others like it stimulated questions about diffusion as a simple, linear process. The "classic" diffusion model could be redefined rather easily to accommodate societal differences in information transfer processes. Structural differences between societies raised some more basic questions about the diffusion model, however. Some questions of this nature are treated in the following section.

SOCIAL STRUCTURE AND THE DIFFUSION PROCESS

The early diffusion studies were based almost exclusively on samples of farmers in the United States. There is no question but that differences in farmers' socioeconomic status were routinely included in the research designs. Differences among farmers in farm size or farm income were found to be related to adoption behavior, documenting that the relatively resource-poor farmer tended to lag behind in adoption of innovations. Differences in control over resources were not considered to be of overwhelming importance in the diffusion process, however, because the relationships with adoption behavior were more or less comparable to the relationships with other kinds of variables.

When the conventional diffusion model was applied in Latin America it became apparent that variability in control over farm resources might be more important, even decisive, in its effect on diffusion.[2] Although scholars such as Loomis (Loomis and McKinney, 1956) had drawn attention to the implications of wide differences in land holdings for action programs in Latin America, there was little empirical basis for estimating the effects of such differences for the diffusion of innovations.

Galjart (1971) was among the first to criticize the conventional approach to diffusion as failing to take social structure fully into account. Galjart had studied technological change processes in Brazil. Against that background he raised serious questions about the rural sociological focus on the individual as decision maker. Galjart (1971) argued that in addition to the emphasis on individuals' lack of knowledge of innovations (the communications emphasis), and differential willingness to adopt (innovativeness), attention should be paid to inability to adopt. In broad terms, Galjart (1971) called for attention to social structure and to the fact that in some contexts large numbers of farmers simply lacked the resources to capitalize on the production potential of technological innovations.

Galjart (1971:38) took an additional step in his reasoning when he said that:

> The failure of rural sociologists and especially diffusion researchers to appreciate the significance of the factor *inability*, that is, the importance of structural, tenure, and infrastructural position, has made them insensitive to the political implications of the work of every extension service, and therefore of their own work.

In the above quotation Galjart (1971) was taking a stand against the conventional diffusion approach. He argued that inability to adopt meant that existing inequalities among farmers would tend to increase. His focus was thus on social structure as a possibly decisive antecedent to adoption and on the structural impact of such adoption as well.

Structural issues are the focus of the following chapter and will not be pursued further here. I chose to introduce the topic here because such questions came up in the context of applying the conventional diffusion model in third world settings. Galjart (1971) challenged the diffusion research tradition in a very fundamental way and that challenge was repeated in the decade of the 1970s and to the present.[3]

CONCLUSIONS

In this chapter I illustrated some facets of the spread of the diffusion research tradition itself to third world settings. Widespread interest in *Transforming Traditional Agriculture* (Schultz, 1964) provided scope for diffusion researchers. Direct transfer of the communications approach at the very least provided useful, local information for purposes of planning action programs. Such practical benefits of research are probably of greater importance in developing countries than in the United States, because agricultural development is more likely to be treated as a planned (and public sector) process. Some questions were also raised about the approach, however, and several of those are illustrated here. Substantial differences in media availability and use, and much lower levels of education among farmers in developing countries, meant that the tactics of information transfer had to be rethought. At a more fundamental level, however, the strategy of reliance on information transfer came to be questioned as awareness of the poverty and powerlessness of many third world farmers increased.

NOTES

1. It is of more than passing interest to note that innovations in public health technology are often disseminated by government decree. The sharp contrast to the voluntaristic methods of dissemination preferred in agriculture should be reminder enough that research strategies are developed in particular value contexts.

2. Apart from the phenomenon of "estate" agriculture, which is commonly oriented to cash crops, the dispersion of land holdings in Asian countries is less than in most Latin American countries.

3. It may or may not be simply coincidence that Galjart, of European background, was less enamored of the socio-psychological approach to research than most American sociologists at that time.

II

RECENT TRENDS

In part II I will describe what has been undertaken by rural sociologists on the topic of diffusion since about 1970. I recognize that it is more than a little arbitrary to designate 1970, even approximately, as a dividing line between that which can be described as more versus less recent. Changes in perspectives about diffusion phenomena have been very gradual. Nevertheless, if I again invoke the trend in articles published in *Rural Sociology* (Christenson and Garkovich, 1985:512), I can make a case for 1970 as a reasonable dividing line between "old" and "new." The ten years from 1966 to 1975 were the peak years for interest in diffusion, with 8.2 percent of all articles in *Rural Sociology* published on that topic. The corresponding percentage for 1976-85 was considerably lower, at 5.4 percent. I expect that pattern of decline to continue into the future but I do not expect interest in diffusion phenomena to disappear. Technological change in the world's agriculture will continue to stimulate interest among rural sociologists. The research approach will be more varied than that reflected in the "classic" model, however, and I think that it was the simplicity of that model that stimulated the surge in popularity of diffusion research in the early years.

In Chapter 4 I will deal with what I regard as a major shift in theoretical perspective that has influenced diffusion research. The poverty of many third world farmers drew attention to a lack of resources as possibly determinant in farmers' ability to adopt modern technology. And coupled with that concern was a further concern with widening existing gaps between rich and poor farmers as a result of using new technologies. The net effect of that type of concern was to shift away from reliance on an approach to understanding diffusion via information transfer to an approach centering on structural antecedents and consequences of adoption.

The general question of consequences of technological change has been dealt with in at least two distinguishable ways by rural sociologists. First, there is the issue of structural consequences: who gains and who loses? And second, there is the question of environmental consequences. Chapter 5 will deal with something of a revival of the earlier popularity of research on diffusion, but with a focus on adoption of an array of conservation-oriented innovations rather than the earlier production-enhancing innovations.

Parenthetically I might mention here that the classic approach to diffusion still has utility with reference to production-oriented innovations, especially in third world settings. In November 1985 I had the opportunity to work for a few weeks at the Agricultural University of the North West Frontier Province in Peshawar, Pakistan. One of the tasks I was asked to undertake was to help in designing a very conventional diffusion survey. The reason for the proposed survey was not to advance scientific knowledge in any profound way, but to obtain detailed information about farmers and farming in one part of the province. In a context in which agricultural research and development is expanding rapidly, and in which researchers and extension workers often lack firsthand knowledge of the agriculture they are trying to transform, it is critical to provide systematic descriptions and analyses of local situations as at least a first step toward familiarizing professional personnel with the concrete problems they are trying to solve. The "classic" model serves well in that role.

In general, however, rural sociologists have shifted away from reliance on the "classic" diffusion model, as I indicated earlier. Another reason for that shift, taken up in Chapter 5, is the recent emphasis on "packages" of innovations and the even more recent "systems" approach to bringing about change in agricultural practices. The systems approach in particular, whether one is dealing with cropping systems or the broader farming systems, has emphasized interdisciplinary efforts and involvement of the farmer and farm family in the research process. The sample survey does not lend itself well to this type of approach and, as I will detail below, it is not clear what rural sociologists can contribute to farming systems research.

I will also describe some recent research which capitalizes on the multiplicity of earlier studies. In at least a few instances, a range of data sets has been aggregated in the interest of testing hypotheses at a more general level than was possible with the typical small sample surveys which have dominated in the diffusion literature. In a sense the many "applied" studies here serve a disciplinary purpose by providing a broader data base than is routinely available in the social sciences.

Finally, in Chapter 6 I will gaze into the proverbial crystal ball. I will list some issues I consider important and in need of resolution. Perhaps one or another of those unresolved issues will attract some research attention.

Recent Trends

4

Social Structure, Equity, and the Diffusion Model

In the preceding chapter I noted that Galjart (1971) had drawn attention to the possibility that many poor farmers in developing countries were simply unable to adopt modern technology. As a consequence, diffusion of such technology and efforts to enhance the rate of diffusion might have political consequences in that the gap between rich and poor could become wider. Though such ideas were not commonly considered at the time it would be a mistake to argue that diffusion research was substantially altered by Galjart's (1971) work or any other particular piece of research. Many other events and changes were taking place at the same time and probably had some impact on research directions.

As background, I should restate the argument that diffusion research had been substantially reoriented toward developing countries. The Bealer and Kling (1975) index of publications in *Rural Sociology* for 1966-75 lists thirty-five substantive articles under the heading of "Adoption" for that period, more than half under the subheading "Outside the U.S." As nearly as I can tell, there were only four articles with a comparable, international classification prior to 1966. Among the reasons for a shift were, as I noted earlier, the efforts of newly independent nations to improve living standards. Another reason, which I can't document, is that interest in diffusion of agricultural innovations declined in the United States as the innovations of the 1940s and 1950s became standard farming practices a decade or two later. As early as the 1950s Cochrane (1958) had described the American farmer as on a technological treadmill. Such imagery was very different from that of the tradition-bound farmer making decisions about novel alternatives.

Still another reason for the upsurge of diffusion research in developing countries was the enormous interest in increased production potential occasioned by the introduction of high-yielding wheat and rice varieties, especially under irrigation. As Saint and Coward (1977) point out, however, some of the early successes of what came to be known as the green revolution seemed to obviate the communications approach. The new technology spread very rapidly without much promotion, where conditions were appropriate for it. And this in turn gave rise to questions about equity with respect to those farmers who, for example, lacked access to assured sources of irrigation water and thus could not share in the production benefits.

In addition to changes having direct implications for agricultural development it is also the case that disciplinary orientations were shifting away from the dominant socio-psychological perspective toward a more structural and macroscopic view of social phenomena. Whereas early diffusion researchers more or less took the existing social system for granted and worked on problems of individual adaptation to the system, what came to be known as a critical perspective in the discipline raised questions about the system itself. Questions about equity were fairly central to the changing disciplinary perspective and such questions influenced diffusion research.

QUESTIONS ABOUT THE DIFFUSION MODEL

Rogers (1976) was highly sensitive to the questions being raised about the classic approach to diffusion and worked toward modifying that model to make it more useful. In particular, Roger (1976) recognized that the tendency to focus research on the farmer as decision-maker contributed to an "individual-blame" type of logic. If one assumes that the farmer is free to decide for or against adoption of an innovation, then it is tempting to find fault with those farmers who do not adopt. The negative overtones of the "laggard" concept fit well here. On the other hand, if the farmer is unable to take action, then it behooves the researcher to consider causal influences beyond the individual. Rogers (1976) suggested that emphasizing information flows was probably an overly narrow perspective. Social structures might have to be modified to permit individuals to act on information received. And, by the same token, if some individuals were not able to respond to the potential of improved technologies, then the perspective of diffusion research would have to be broadened to consider consequences for the individual and for society as well.

Goss (1979) published another critique of the conventional diffusion model. To briefly summarize, Goss argued that the main limitations of diffusion theory are its individualistic, psychological bias and its assumption of fairness in the distribution of the benefits that accrue from the diffusion process. This criticism was derived from Havens (1975) and Havens and Flinn (1975). They argued, first, that the existing institutional and structural arrangements, into which technological innovations are introduced, create constraints on the distribution of benefits; and, second, that degree of access or influence over economic institutions effectively determines the consequences for individuals and, social systems.

Goss (1979) argued that the classic diffusion model also errs in its narrow approach to consequences of an innovation for the social system and individuals in the social system. It ignores the broader range of unanticipated consequences. Finally, Goss proposed a framework for the study of the consequences of diffusion of innovations (not just for the immediate client system, but for the larger social systems as well), in which both the level and the distribution of consequences are measured as dependent variables. Besides focusing on the consequences of technological change in agriculture, the critique drew on empirical research to document the argument. Goss (1979) cited data from a study by Havens and Flinn (1975) on coffee production technology in Colombia, and another study by Gotsch (1972) concerned with tubewell irrigation in Bangladesh and Pakistan.

Havens and Flinn (1975) were able to trace the consequences of introducing improved production technology among Colombian coffee growers over a seven-year period, from 1963 to 1970. While their sample size was small—only fifty-six individuals were contacted at both time points—the longitudinal dimension permitted them to pin down consequences. The critical element in technological change was the introduction of new plant material, coffee trees with greater production potential. By 1970 only 30 percent of the sample had adopted the new plant material. The main reasons for non-adoption hinged on credit availability. Changing from one coffee variety to another involves a waiting period of at least three years for the new planting to produce. A grower who switched varieties would therefore have to forego income from production on replanted land for a substantial time, and the need for credit becomes apparent. Not all growers had access to credit, however. While both adopters and non-adopters of the new variety increased production and income per acre between 1963 and 1970, the adopters increased more. As a consequence, the adopters acquired more land while the non-adopters, on average, reduced acreage. In short, some growers were able to benefit from the new technology while others were not, with strong implications that control over land was shifting toward the minority of adopters.

Gotsch (1972) did a similar, though cross-sectional, analysis of adoption of tubewell irrigation. A sample of farmers with 1 to 2.5 acres of land in Bangladesh was compared with a sample in Pakistan with farms averaging between 7.5 and 12.5 acres. Gotsch (1972) demonstrated that the farmers with larger holdings were more likely to put in tubewells and were thus better able to capitalize on the production potential of the new seed varieties, which must have adequate water to reach their potential. Though no lapse in production is involved in this example, credit is again implicated. A tubewell is by definition a deep well and putting in place such a well requires a considerable capital outlay. Access to credit is critical. In addition, the farmer with only a small amount of land, say one acre, could ordinarily not justify the investment for that farm alone, even if credit were available, since the typical well can produce water enough for several acres.

Goss (1979) used the analyses described above and other citations to argue for a shift away from the socio-psychological approach to diffusion in the direction of a sociological and macro-level approach, so that constraints to adoption outside the individual could receive appropriate attention. At the same time he called for a shift in emphasis in diffusion research to focus on consequences, as the ultimate variable to be explained. The topic of consequences, in particular, has received a good deal of attention in recent years. In the following paragraphs I will review some of that material with the objective of clarifying what is known and not known at this stage.

THE CONSEQUENCES OF TECHNOLOGICAL CHANGE: IDENTIFYING THE ISSUES

If the great promise of the green revolution and other factors led to some rethinking of the diffusion process, later reactions to the actual effects of high-yielding varieties also contributed to the tendency to reject the entire approach. The general assumption that benefits would "trickle down" to the most needy came to be viewed with a great deal of suspicion. The world's food needs were not met at one stroke, though supplies of certain commodities had increased sharply. Hunger remained a problem, though not as widespread as a generation earlier. Diffusion research did ignore equity questions in the early years, but I think that there has been an over-reaction to the equity question that fails to take account of the facts. World agriculture supplies food for a constantly increasing population and average life expectancies are also increasing. That leaves plenty of room for inequities, and these need to be analyzed, but the picture is not all bleak.

My concern here is not with development as a whole, however, but with the more narrow topic of the distributive effect of technological change in agriculture. By and large I am of the opinion that rural sociologists have over-reacted to illustrations of inequitable effects and have been lax in doing the research necessary to specify impact questions.

Goss' (1979) call for attention to the consequences of technological change has merit. A qualifying point he did not make, however, might have drawn attention to the fact that the empirical data he cited had to do with capital intensive innovations. Introducing a new coffee variety involves investment capital for the seedlings, the cost of removing old trees and preparing for the new planting, the normal cost for fertilizer and pest control, plus foregoing income for at least three years on the replanted land. The smallholder is at a disadvantage in adopting a capital intensive technology such as changing coffee or other tree crop varieties.

Similarly, as I pointed out earlier, the smallholder is at a disadvantage in adopting tubewell irrigation. Drilling a deep well, installing the necessary casing for the well, and installing a pump are all relatively expensive. Tubewell irrigation is attractive in areas that have groundwater supplies but lack canal irrigation, in that it can assure the farmer of water when needed for a given crop and can also permit double- or triple-cropping. Smallholders are at a disadvantage in acquiring the necessary capital, however, and may well have to combine forces with neighboring farmers to justify and fully utilize a deep well.

The above examples both illustrate situations where inability to adopt an improved technology can result in both short- and long-term negative consequences for some farmers. Not all of the improved technology theoretically available to farmers is of a capital intensive nature, however. In fact, at a global level, the bulk of the production-enhancing technology does not require a substantial capital investment.

THE CONSEQUENCES OF TECHNOLOGICAL CHANGE: DISCUSSION OF THE ISSUES

The first of the issues to be addressed in assessing the consequences of technological change has to do with capital intensity. A concise way to specify the issues is to pose the questions in terms of *scale neutrality*. To what degree is adoption of an innovation dependent on the size of the farm enterprise? A second and related issue has to do with mechanization. By and large mechanical innovations require significant capital outlays. Thus they are often not scale neutral. A more important characteristic of mechanical innovations, however, is that they are *labor saving*, while chemical and genetic innovations as well as cultural practices tend to be *land saving*. The relative availability of land versus labor thus becomes a central question.

Both of the above issues are discussed briefly later. They merit extensive discussion, but by and large the research that has a bearing on the issues comes from disciplines other than sociology or rural sociology and is not directly tied to diffusion; thus it is outside the scope of this monograph. My intent is to draw attention to the issues in hopes that sociological research can be directed to them.

One further issue must be specified if sociological research on the consequences of technological change is to be productive. It is important to be clear about which segments of a population are affected in which ways by technological change. Rural sociologists have tended to focus on equity issues related to farm size; that is, the discussion has tended to focus on farmers only. Very little work has been done on farm labor, on farm producers versus urban consumers, on gender issues, and on differential impacts across regions. A considerably broader perspective is appropriate, as will be argued below.

Scale neutrality or the lack of it is an important issue in specifying the consequences of technological change. Much of the improved technology introduced to world agriculture is at least arguably scale neutral. The high-yielding varieties of rice, wheat, corn, and some other crops can be planted by small and large farmers alike. Cash for the purchase of improved seed to replace seed traditionally held over from an earlier crop can be an obstacle, but seed purchases can be broken down to very small quantities to offset the need for cash. Much the same thing can be said about chemical fertilizers, insecticides, and herbicides. Tubewells and tractors cannot be broken down into small units to accommodate the financial capacity of the smallholder, but genetic and chemical innovations, by and large, can be applied to a square meter of land about as readily as to a larger area.

Apart from theory, the available data also support the idea that modern plant materials and chemical inputs are scale neutral in their effects. It is true that smallholders generally are relatively slow in adopting innovations. The size-related adoption lag is not a continuing disadvantage, however. A study by Shingi et al. (1981) is one of the few longitudinal studies on this issue and documents, for one area, that the status of laggard is not permanent. Cross-sectional studies, largely from the economics literature, make essentially the same point. Smallholders, who tend to be late in adopting innovations, show productivity gains which can be attributed to improved plant materials to about the same extent as large farmers (e.g., Sidhu, 1974, on wheat; Swenson, 1976, on rice). Ruttan (1977) summarizes a range of studies on the impact of high-yielding varieties and concludes that neither farm size nor tenure are obstacles to adoption. Early lags in adoption are made up in a relatively short time. Furthermore, Ruttan (1977) concludes that neither farm size nor tenure leads to differential growth in productivity.

I am willing to accept the proposition that modern crop varieties are, on the whole, scale neutral. Their diffusion does not contribute to increased inequality (nor is the impact redistributive or contributory to reducing inequality). Some important qualifications must be added so that research on equity issues can move in productive directions. I cited the Havens and Flinn (1975) study earlier as an example of the higher capital requirements that can be involved in introducing a new variety of tree crop. Access to irrigation water is probably a more important constraint for smallholders, as was indicated for tubewells (Gotsch, 1972; see also Frankel, 1971). The smallholder may also be at a disadvantage in canal irrigation systems to the extent that location on the system can leave some farmers without water when needed and, more importantly, to the extent that differentials in power among water users on the same canal can contribute to differences in services.[1] In situations in which access to irrigation water is a constraint, and to the extent that such access is not scale neutral, it would follow that smallholders will be disadvantaged in the use of seed-fertilizer technology as well.

At the risk of digressing unduly, it may also be worth mentioning here that although rural sociologists (myself included) frequently invoke a need for credit, we apparently ignore research on credit availability or the functioning of credit institutions. The list of subject headings in the recent fifty-year index of *Rural Sociology* (Garkovich, 1985:142) moves inexorably from Costa Rica to Crime, with no intervening heading for credit. Meanwhile, agricultural economists of course do concern themselves with credit. And some of those economists challenge what seems to be an implicit assumption among rural sociologists that public sector credit programs will encourage more nearly equitable agricultural development (for a review see Adams and Vogel, 1986). Credit, or the lack of credit, becomes something of a "black box" in rural sociological research, cited as a probable cause for some phenomenon without benefit of investigation.

My main point in listing some qualifications above—and there probably are others that should be listed-is to indicate that there are circumstances in which scale neutrality is an issue in diffusion of modern plant varieties. Such circumstances, including credit issues, should be the object of research. In general, I strongly suspect that introducing modern plant materials has much more impact on regional inequality than on intra-regional inequality among individual farmers, however. This is a topic to which I will return later.

Mechanization, or the adoption of mechanical innovations, is in general not scale neutral. Most mechanical innovations involve sizable capital outlays and for that reason are more accessible to farmers with relatively large land holding. It is not obvious that any advantage that accrues to operators of larger farms increases existing inequality among large versus small farm operators, however. Machines substitute for animal power or human labor, but have little if any impact on the productivity of land.[2] Pumps are an exception in that they bring another critical input, water, to the land. Machines can improve the precision of seeding operations or application of fertilizer, and they can improve the timeliness of task performance. The latter can be a factor in shifting from two to three crops per year, for example. Machines can thus indirectly affect volume of production from a given piece of land, but do not directly increase productivity of the land.

The introduction of modern crop technology in the developing countries has increased demand for labor (Ruttan, 1977). Garg and Srivastava (1972) illustrate the increase with data from 100 farms (in India) over a five-year period, from 1966 through 1971. During that time the crop acreage seeded to high-yielding varieties increased from 11 percent of the total acreage to 35 percent. Labor inputs increased from 93 days of human labor per hectare to 146 days per hectare over the same time period. Increases in labor inputs were about the same regardless of farm size, though in general the proportion of total labor hired increased. Barnes and Vanneman (1983) analyzed 1961 and 1971 census data for all of India to make the same point at a more general level. They went on to analyze the relationship between production increases over time and the status of farm workers. Barnes and Vanneman (1983:103-105) concluded that increased labor demand was met by increases in hired labor in the short term, but that in the long term the number of self-employed cultivators increased proportionately. Production gains, therefore, did not lead to increased proletarianization of smallholders.

The above materials were cited as background for making several more general points. First, for much of the third world, agricultural development has focused on crop production technology that enhances productivity of the land. Second, such technology has increased demand for labor. Third, labor displacing technologies such as tractors have not been much of an issue for the simple reason that labor is cheap relative to machines.[3] Fourth, there is the possibility that land-enhancing technology can contribute to increasing inequality between small and large farmers, but a substantial amount of data would tend to argue against that possibility. Much more research is needed and impacts may very well be location-specific. The most important issue, in my opinion, has little to do with mechanization or farm size but does involve the extent to which hired farm labor shares in the benefits of production increases. Rural sociologists have largely ignored this issue in third world settings.

Research on mechanization in developed countries, especially the United States, has received some attention from rural sociologists in the last few years. Berardi and Geisler's (1984) recent volume on the consequences of technological change is almost entirely concerned with the impact of mechanization. The several chapters in that volume make a good start on mapping out some of the complexities of impact issues: impacts on small versus large farmers, farmers versus hired laborers, male versus female laborers, alien versus domestic laborers, regional impacts, and so on.[4]

Stockdale (1977) warned that a replay of the role that mechanization had in transforming U.S. agriculture in developing countries could have serious equity consequences. The warning should be taken seriously. Many of those countries still have most of their total labor forces involved in agriculture, with little prospect for alternative employment. By the same token, however, to the extent that farm labor is readily available, it is unlikely that mechanization will proceed rapidly in such situations. By and large mechanical innovations have had their origin in the private sector (Binswanger, 1984).[5] With cheap labor there has been little incentive to introduce machines. This is in sharp contrast to the demand for technologies that directly increase food production. The latter technologies are generated in the public sector, for the most part, and for that reason are at least theoretically more amenable to control. Prior to discussing control measures, however, it is essential to identify where impacts occur.

Who is impacted by technological change? As I indicated above, rural sociologists have tended to focus on farm-size differentials in discussing impact questions. This is understandable in view of the structural changes that have taken place in the agricultural industries of the developed countries. The extreme inequities of resource distribution in much of Latin America also contribute to the focus on farm-size differentials.[6] In much of Asia and Africa, on the other hand, there is room for arguing that an emphasis on regional and other differentials should have top priority. Lipton and Longhurst (1985:23) go so far as to state that "at least 90 percent of the *literature* on 'what [modern varieties] do to the poor' is about small farmers and tenants in [regions where the modern varieties are grown]." Yet, they argue, as much as 90 percent "of the *effects* of modern varieties on poverty and income distribution are via availability and price of consumed food and via impact on poor farmers in (regions that do not grow modern varieties)." Parenthetically I might note here that almost all of the literature cited by Lipton and Longhurst (1985) in their extensive review is from disciplines other than sociology, primarily economics.

Regional differentials are important for the simple reason that agroclimatic conditions are variable and the production enhancing technology that is sweeping world agriculture tends to be location specific. Hybrid corn increased corn production dramatically, but that benefit was not shared by farmers in the many parts of the world where corn will not do well or where food preferences favored other crops. The same thing can be said for wheat and rice and other crops (and animal species) for which improved technology has been generated. A technological breakthrough will have uneven impacts because of diversity in the resource base and in societal preferences. The establishment of an array of International Agricultural Research Centers (IARCs) in recent years represents a major step toward addressing location-specific production problems. But that step alone cannot guarantee technologies which are appropriate for the diverse agroclimatic conditions that characterize world agriculture, nor can that step guarantee equitable results.

I think that there is scope for rural sociologists to do comparative studies that can help to specify the nature of regional inequities. Agroclimatic conditions are of major importance but food preferences, institutional constraints—for example, constraints on organizing smallholders to pooling of resources in irrigation systems—and an array of other factors are important as well. All of this has very little to do with diffusion research in the narrow sense, but it has a great deal to do with understanding technological change processes.

If the consequences of technological change are to be the ultimate variable to be explained, as Goss (1979) suggested, then those consequences must first be specified. A second step would be to assess the option for redressing the inequities that have been identified. Survey research will not be very helpful here, but I suspect that the approaches of political sociology can be useful. A recent paper by Buttel (1983), entitles "Beyond the Family Farm," can serve to illustrate the point. To me that paper said that the structure of American agriculture had changed and that reverting to the pattern of an earlier generation was not likely to happen. The author essentially asked: What are the options, what are the trade-offs, what are the probabilities that one or another line of action could achieve a desired end? It is questions of that order that must be addressed. In the context of regional inequities this means, among other things, that questions of research policy must be raised, and the trade-off between equity and efficiency must be squarely addressed. If development resources were infinite one could avoid such questions, but that is not the case.

Beyond the matter of regional inequities, I believe that it is important to gain a better understanding of the impacts of technological change on other than the farm operator and farm firm. Given the increased labor requirements of improved technology in many developing countries, to what extent does labor share in the benefit of production gains? Under what circumstances is it likely that machinery may substitute for human labor? It may or may not be possible to institutionalize the kind of social impact assessment procedure that Friedland (1984) has suggested, but it should be possible to *anticipate* impacts on farm labor to a degree.

Urban consumers, especially the poor, are of course also impacted by production gains. To this point rural sociologists have been content to let economists assess impacts of food production differentials and prices on urban consumers. Unfortunately that contributes to an overly narrow specification of impacts among rural sociologists, that is, the small-farm versus large-farm focus. Technologies that may have different impacts for males and females are also important, especially in African societies where women play a prominent role in agricultural production. Other constituencies could undoubtedly be listed. My purpose here, however, is to stress two more general points. First, it is important to extend research on technological change to the consideration of consequences of such change. And second, in specifying consequences, it is critical to consider consequences for farmers and other segments of society as well, both rural and urban. I believe that an approach to impact questions from a macro-level perspective can be productive.

SUMMARY AND CONCLUSIONS

In this chapter I have traced the origins of a major challenge to diffusion research. From an early recognition of resource differentials so extreme as to prohibit adoption of improved technology, to a later and more widespread concern with differential consequences of adoption, the classic diffusion model was challenged and found wanting. The classic model had always included resource differentials as antecedents of adoption, though the potential importance of such differentials was not apparent until diffusion studies were carried out in developing countries. And the classic diffusion model could at least theoretically be extended to focus on the consequences of adoption as the ultimate variable to be explained. For a variety of reasons the classic diffusion model has not simply been extended. Among those reasons is a general shift in the discipline of sociology from a dominantly micro-level approach to research to a more structural, macro-level approach. At the more abstract level, the broader issues of technological change and agricultural development have been favored over questions concerned with individual farmers' decision-making.

In the body of the chapter I argued that both farmers' adoption of technology and the consequences of differential adoption must deal with at least three issues: scale neutrality, the labor displacing quality of mechanical technology, and the question of impacts beyond the farmer alone. Implicitly I argued that structural transformation of the world's agriculture is not a necessary consequence of increasing capital intensity. The degree of capital intensity must be considered, and the availability and price of farm labor must be considered as well. At the same time I also called for broader investigation of the impacts of technological change so that equity questions could be objectively specified and ultimately addressed in policy terms.

While I believe that the treatment of equity issues has shifted attention away from diffusion processes as such, diffusion research is not likely to disappear from the scene. As I indicated earlier, even the narrowly focused communications approach still has utility in mapping out the terrain in areas where modern technology is still largely unknown. And in the following chapter I will discuss several areas in which diffusion processes are being or can be studied by rural sociologists.

NOTES

1. Freeman et al. (1982) analyze power differentials among water users in a canal irrigation system as related to adoption of innovations. They used a reputational measure of power without explicit reference to differences in farm size or other status factors, thus their study is not directly relevant here, but it does highlight power as an issue.

2. Binswanger (1984) provides an excellent overview of this topic and provides supportive data.
3. There are exceptions. Binswanger (1984) cites Brazil and Pakistan as instances in which government policy has favored mechanization to the disadvantage of farm labor.
4. A report prepared by a task force brought together by the Council for Agricultural Science and Technology (CAST, 1983), a task force chaired by James H. Copp, is also relevant here. The task force concluded, among other things, that many questions about the social impact of agricultural mechanization could not be answered in view of the dearth of data. (See also Copp, 1984.)
5. The CAST (1983) report also notes that some mechanical innovations, such as center-pivot irrigation systems, stem from farmers themselves. See also Carlson, et al. (1987) for the development of a functional no-till drill in the Palouse.
6. Though in much of Latin America the poor are concentrated in towns and cities.

5

Recent Diffusion Research: Some New Directions

Rural sociologists are currently involved in a substantial amount of diffusion research, perhaps more than in the recent past. As a crude measure of current interest one might take note of the number of papers on adoption/diffusion at the 1986 annual meetings of the Rural Sociological Society, held in Salt Lake City. My count of such papers yielded a total of fourteen dealing with adoption and diffusion in five separate paper sessions. Two of the five sessions were exclusively devoted to the topic. In contrast, my perusal of titles of papers presented ten years earlier, at the 1976 RSS meetings held in New York, identified only one paper reporting diffusion research, and that in a session oriented to a broader topic.

At the risk of attributing too much meaning to a crude count on titles of papers, I will also note here that ten of the fourteen papers of diffusion topics presented at the 1986 annual meetings dealt with the diffusion of conservation and resource preservation technology and practices. There is little question but that the diffusion of conservation practices is attracting some attention among rural sociologists, and I will describe in some detail the soil conservation research in the next section. In succeeding sections I will address other current research on diffusion, such as the relationship of capital use to environmental practices, some of which builds rather directly on the older research tradition and some of which departs from that tradition.

DIFFUSION RESEARCH AND THE ENVIRONMENT

It is rather difficult to characterize rural sociologists' research on diffusion as related to environmental issues, largely for the obvious reason that the research emphasis is fairly recent and a number of questions remain open to debate. As stated by van Es (1983:77), "resource-protection issues are consequences of the technological transformation in agriculture." In the latter sense the current research can be viewed as a second generation phenomenon. A vast array of genetic, chemical, mechanical, and managerial innovations has been incorporated into contemporary agriculture, and some of the consequences of that transformation are viewed as less than environmentally benign. The question then is, what can be done to correct that situation?

Another type of question is also being raised, however. Given variability in ecological conditions, why not incorporate ecological constraints into research models intended to address diffusion problems in order to better understand the process itself? The transformation of agriculture is a continuing process, in other words, and one of the gaps in our knowledge of that process involves the failure to consider ecological constraints on the diffusion of innovations. From that perspective it is but a small step to raise questions about the appropriateness of existing technology for the array of both ecological and social conditions extant in world agriculture.

In the following paragraphs I describe diffusion research related to environmental concerns in terms of three categories of questions— questions related to the broad themes I have sketched out above. The categories are neither mutually exclusive nor exhaustive, but they may serve to organize discussion of a currently active and changing research area. The first category of questions has to do with the appropriateness of the traditional diffusion model for analysis of diffusion of conservation practices. The second category of questions deals with the hypothesis that intensification of the production process and the structure of the industry itself *necessarily* lead to exploitation of the natural resource base. The third is a category of questions about the utility of introducing ecological variability into diffusion research designs, that is, the "appropriate technology" theme.

Is the "classic" model appropriate for analyzing the diffusion of conservation practices? Pampel and van Es (1977) tested the proposition that a set of farmer characteristics derived from the conventional approach to diffusion would be more successful in predicting adoption of production-enhancing (commercial) innovations than in predicting adoption of soil conservation (environmental) innovations. A basic element in their reasoning is that the bulk of the technology introduced into agriculture in the past forty or so years was intended to increase production and/or productivity. The presumed beneficiary is thus the farmer, at least in the short run. Voluntarism or, put differently, action based on self-interest, an important part of the theoretical underpinning of the classic diffusion model, is consistent with the rationale for introducing production-enhancing technology. Soil conservation technology, on the other hand, is intended to benefit future generations, and in a more immediate sense, society at large, by conserving the land resource and reducing sediment and chemical deposits in streams, lakes, and reservoirs. Thus, Pampel and van Es (1977) argue, the classic diffusion model (or variants of the same) should not be expected to predict innovativeness with respect to soil conservation practices.

Pampel and van Es (1977) took the line of reasoning indicated above a step farther in testing their ideas. They recognized that some commercial innovations are likely to be more profitable to the farmer than others and that some environmental innovations may be immediately profitable while others are not. Drawing on past research on attributes of innovations (described in an earlier chapter), they obtained ratings of perceived profitability from farmer respondents for nine innovations they classified as commercial and six innovations classified as environmental. Then, after factor analyzing a matrix of the intercorrelations of adoption of all fifteen of the innovations (see the discussion centering on Table 1, Chapter 2), they determined that innovativeness could *not* be treated as a single dimension (Pampel and van Es, 1977:66). Having made that determination, they constructed four separate indexes of innovativeness, directed toward commercial more and less profitable innovations and environmental more and less profitable innovations. Finally, they justified the use of the four separate indexes by factor analyzing the intercorrelations among the indexes and then regressed the indexes on measures of a set of farm and farmer characteristics (Pampel and van Es, 1977:67-68). From the latter analysis they concluded that such variables as farm size and farmer's education best served to predict innovativeness with respect to the more profitable, commercial innovations. Adoption of the least profitable environmental innovations was least well predicted by the same set of farm and farmer characteristics, and thus their argument was supported by the data.

Nowak (1983) is among those who take the position that the conventional approach to diffusion can be useful in analyzing the adoption and diffusion of conservation practices, though some modifications of the model may be necessary. Before turning to the suggested modifications, it may be appropriate to highlight what might me called a philosophical difference among researchers concerned about agricultural technology and the environment. Nowak (1983:83) takes the position that the "conservation does not pay" argument has been overstated. If one accepts the non-profitability position, Nowak (1983:83) argues, then it follows that the implicit voluntarism of the classic, communications-oriented diffusion model is not very useful. Further, if voluntary adoption of conservation technology is not to be expected, then the use of incentives to encourage adoption and mandatory compliance strategies are called for, and these have not been very effective, Nowak argues (1983:83). Van Es (1983:81), on the other hand, takes the position that rural sociologists' insistence on use of the traditional diffusion model, assuming voluntary adoption for private gain, threatens to legitimize a "politically preferred approach to resource protection not because the research strongly supports the efficacy of the policy, but because it is the only policy approach about which the research has anything to say."

I doubt that the debate over who gains from adoption of resource-conserving technology and the accompanying debate over appropriate diffusion strategies is likely to be settled soon. An immediate reason for my doubt is that, for a given technology, the issue of profitability is not a constant. As Buttel et al. (1986:351) point out, in the current period of farm financial stress "many farmers have become dissatisfied with prevailing agricultural practices because of the large cash outlays that are required for inputs." The resource-conserving practice of reduced tillage, for example, may well be more attractive in an era of low commodity prices than it would otherwise have been because it reduces outlays for fuel.

Nowak's (1983) suggestions for modifications in the traditional approach to diffusion also address issues raised in the debate over appropriate diffusion strategies that I have sketched out above. Figure 5, taken from Nowak (1983), outlines a research strategy substantially different from the socio-psychologically oriented, linear, and communications approach that dominated early research on diffusion.

In Figure 5 Nowak (1983) draws attention to both micro and macro influences on farmers' actions, thus explicitly rejecting the heavily voluntaristic flavor of earlier work. Although it is not clear how many aspects of the approach presented in Figure 5 might be operationally defined, Nowak (1983) makes allowance for incentives, regulations, and market factors to influence the decision to adopt

Figure 5
Micro/Macro Influences on the Use of Conservation Practices

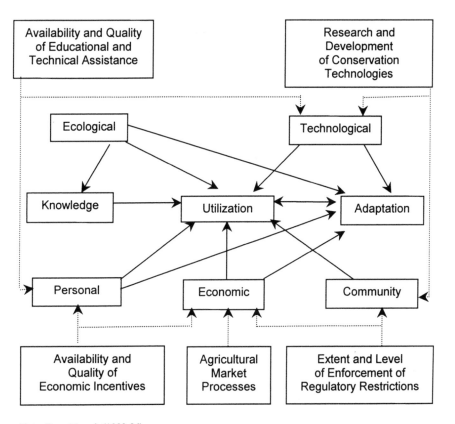

Note: From Nowak (1983:86)

conservation practices, as shown at the bottom of Figure 5. The broad questions as to who gains from conservation technology and the choice of an appropriate diffusion strategy are therefore on the research agenda.

Several more direct modifications of the traditional diffusion model are embodied in Nowak's (1983) discussion of the knowledge-utilization-adaptation sequence depicted in the middle of Figure 5. Nowak (1983:87-88) argues that the traditional view of the adoption process as progressing from awareness to recognition of a problem and eventual adoption (see Chapter 2) is useful, but that knowledge of the subtle nature of much soil erosion is often lacking among farmers. Furthermore, he argues that the complex interactions between erosion, productivity, and soil conservation technology in particular settings is not well understood by scientists, much less those who use the land. In short, the adequacy of available knowledge is perhaps more problematic than has been realized by those doing research on conservation technology.

In addition, Nowak (1983:88) argues that the conventional techniques for assessing utilization of a technology, often involving no more than a yes or no response, are inadequate with respect to conservation technology. "Relative to erosion processes, we need to know where these technologies are being used and the extent to which they are being utilized" (Nowak 1983:88). The general issue of effective or optimal use of technology has by and large been ignored by diffusion research, and I assume that this can be attributed to the strong emphasis on aggregating indicators of adoption into measures of a presumed personality trait, innovativeness. Nowak (1983) is not alone in taking the position that soil and water conservation technologies are appropriate or inappropriate depending on highly localized soil, slope, and other conditions. And along the same lines, Nowak (1983:88-89) also argues that conservation technologies are often adapted to specific problem situations. Utilization and adaptation are therefore linked by a two-way arrow in Figure 5 to depict a rather dynamic and quite possibly idiosyncratic trial and error process in arriving at the solution to a particular problem.

In summary, several of the suggested modifications to the conventional approach to diffusion of innovations indicated in Figure 5 center on the idea that soil erosion and erosion control are not discrete phenomena. Soil erosion takes various forms, depending on local conditions, and erosion control is not achievable through adoption of some single innovation in a widely applicable form. Debates about the utility of focusing on certain types of technology, about ways of measuring adoption behavior, and about constraints on voluntary action are not new to the diffusion research tradition. That research on the diffusion of resource-conserving technology is being pursued, and that elements of the traditional approach are under debate, suggest that a research tradition continues to be viable. That is not to say that current research on diffusion is or should be carried out in terms of some highly defined "model," set for all time. That was not the case in past decades and is not the case now.

A good illustration of *both* continuity and change in diffusion research as it applies to control of soil erosion is provided by Carlson and Dillman's (1983) research in the substantially erosion-prone Palouse region of eastern Washington. These authors propose that farming arrangements involving close relatives (e.g., father and son) will be more innovative with respect to soil conservation practices than non-kin arrangements, because of the implied intergenerational transfer of the farm property. They thus contribute to the modest accumulation of research on family and kin factors that may affect adoption. Carlson and Dillman's approach to diffusion is basically in keeping with the older tradition, but they do not include attitudinal or communications variables in their design and that is a departure from the "classic" model. Similarly, they maintain a distinction between conservation and other technology and that is consistent with a fairly recent development.

The continuity of their research with classical diffusion theory, however, is shown in their more recent papers. For example, in Carlson et al. (1987), they trace the use of the no-till drill, developed by an innovative farmer, and examine the context of the innovation, the nature of the innovation, and the characteristics of individual adopters. Adopters of no-till technology were more likely to be attitudinally convinced that erosion was a problem; but economics played an even greater influential role in adoption. Carlson et al. (1987) concluded that a two-way information flow between farmers and researchers is essential for further advances in technology and effective use by farmers.

In another study, Carlson and Dillman (1988) show that farmers' mechanical skills contributed to first use and adoption of no-till technology. In the most recent unpublished study, Carlson et al. (1992) report on a follow-up survey to determine changes in attitudes and behaviors from 1976 to 1990. They conclude that the positive trend in use of conservation practices is a result of changes in the context, that is, societal pressures and regulations to reduce erosion, and characteristics of farmers. Younger and better educated farmers are aware and willing to adopt technologies to reduce erosion.

Carlson and Dillman's (1983) research results support the idea that farmers who operate farms with close kin are more innovative with respect to erosion control technology but not other types of technology. In a substantial replication of the Palouse study, however, van Es and Tsoukalas (1987) presented data that did not support the hypothesized linkage between kin ties and adoption of erosion control practices. These authors obtained data from crop farmers in what they refer to as a "prairie" setting (essentially a statewide sample from Illinois). They argue that in absence of soil erosion as a perceived threat to productivity, farming with kin will not be conducive to adoption of soil conservation technology, and their data support that argument. Substantial soil loss due to erosion can be demonstrated in both settings, but perceptions of this loss as an actual threat to productivity may well differ. The latter idea ties back to Nowak's (1983; 1987) point that the complexities of both soil loss and its control are not well understood. This raises questions about the presumed link between knowledge and adoption, which has been part of the traditional approach to diffusion and economics of adoption (see the discussion about Figure 5, above), and suggests another area for change in the approach.

Does increasing capital intensity necessarily lead to exploitive use of natural resources? The preceding is the second of the general questions I have chosen as an aid in describing some of the current research on technology as related to environmental issues. Increasing capital intensity, in this context, is not only concerned with major capital investments in agricultural production, including land purchase, but also with the routine use of capital to purchase production inputs rather than rely on home-produced inputs. Capital concentration, especially in the form of land, is also a matter of concern.

Heffernan and Green (1986) express some doubt about the theoretical relevance of the traditional approach to diffusion for research on diffusion of soil conservation technology. The bulk of the research within that tradition supported the general proposition that higher socioeconomic status was conducive to early adoption of innovations. It was in fact a recognition of some possible implications of those consistent research findings that led to the concern about smallholders' inability to adopt improved technology and the long-run equity implications of that inability, as discussed in Chapter 4. Heffernan and Green (1986:34) suggest that precisely opposite results might also be expected with reference to adoption of resource-conserving practices, that is, that "small-scale farmers preserve the environment better than large-scale farmers because the capital intensive technologies large-scale farmers use force them to take a short-term view of their farming operation."

In their research Heffernan and Green (1986) neither accept the posture of traditional diffusion research, that large-scale farmers should be more ready to adopt, nor the ecological critique of that approach, that large-scale farmers are constrained to be exploitive of the resource base. Instead, they test a proposition that lies somewhere between the two extremes: large-scale farmers may well have less erosion-prone land, thus less need for control measures and, as a result, less soil loss. Land quality, in other words, is posed as a critical factor in accounting for variability in soil loss rather than farm size.

Heffernan and Green (1986) test their ideas with data from 120 crop farmers in a single county. With the use of soil maps they derived an independent measure of erosion potential for each field in a given sample farm. Then, with detailed data from interviews concerning cropping practices on those fields and tillage practices employed, they derived estimates of actual soil loss. These field-specific data were then combined to derive weighted averages of soil-loss potential and estimated loss for the whole farm. Their data analysis demonstrated that larger scale farms tended to have less soil-loss potential and lower estimated loss, as they had expected. Finally, using a regression analysis, they determined that farm size (measured as gross farm sales) was not positively (nor significantly) associated with estimated soil loss, thus confirming the results of the simple correlation analysis described above. Erosion potential, which is higher for small farms, is cited as the best predictor of estimated soil loss.

A recent essay by Walter Firey (1984) makes an argument that is similar to the Heffernan and Green (1986) argument described above in several respects. Firey (1984) suggests, in part, that the farmer's financial security should be treated as intervening between farm size and measures of exploitive versus conservative resource use. Whether the farm operation is large or small, that is to say, the individual who is more financially secure should tend to be less exploitive in his/her use of resources. Heffernan and Green's (1986:38) finding that a high ratio of total worth to debt is negatively (but not significantly) associated with estimated soil loss supports the above reasoning. Also supportive is the Buttel et al. (1981) finding that farmers with a high net worth tend to have attitudes more favorable toward soil conservation quite apart from differences in farm size (measured as gross farm income).

I doubt that the research done thus far can sustain any firm conclusions about the relationship, if any, between capital concentration and exploitive or nonexploitive use of natural resources in agriculture. It is my opinion that the superficially plausible hypothesis that small-scale (and thus presumably "family") farmers are more likely to be "good stewards" of the soil can not be sustained. At the very least such possibly intervening variables as differential control of high-quality land and financial security may have to be taken into account. Some other recent research has at least a tangential bearing on the general question, however. Albrecht and Thomas (1986) recently published an elaborate treatment of farm tenure as a factor in adoption of conservation practices. And Dillman and Carlson (1982) have explored the role of landlords toward the same end. Both of these studies, and I hope some future research as well, will help to solidify the research base.

I must say that I was intrigued by the Albrecht and Thomas (1986) study of the relationship between farm tenure and adoption of practices because it addressed some stubbornly held views. A full generation ago Lionberger (1960:101-102) had indicated that the relationship between tenancy and adoption of innovations was likely to be complex because of regional differences in tenancy arrangements and individual differences in landlord-tenant relationships. As the capital intensity of agriculture increased, especially in the industrialized countries, it was generally recognized that the prudent farm operator had little choice but to allocate increasing amounts of scarce capital to machinery and production-input purchases, thus reducing the emphasis on land ownership. And yet the long-held view that tenancy was at best a step toward ownership and at worst a hallmark of shiftlessness has, if not prevailed, persisted.

Albrecht and Thomas (1986:21) obtained data from a representative, statewide sample of Texas crop producers (N=452).

Rather than use a nominal measure of tenure, as has been customary, Albrecht and Thomas (1986:22) devised a continuous variable expressed as the percentage of all land in the farm owned by the respondent. That variable was then regressed on the variables listed in Table 7.

It is apparent from Table 7 that respondents in the Texas sample who owned most or all of their land were *not* more likely to adopt soil conservation practices than respondents who owned little or none of their farmland. The relationship indicated in Table 7 is not significant

Table 7
Regression Coefficients Indicating the Relationships Between Percentages of Farmland Owned and Other Variables, with Farm Size (in Acres) and Age of Respondent Controlled

	Standardized regression coefficients
Gross farm sales	-.15*
Days of off-farm employment	.24*
Percentage of income from farming	-.25*
Adoption of:	
Soil conservation practices	-.06
Farm financial practices	-.10*
Community involvement	-.06
Education	.13*

Note: From Albrecht and Thomas (1986:25).

* Significant at .05 level

and, perhaps more importantly, is negative (-.06). Adoption of soil conservation practices was measured by a simple count of the number of six possible conservation techniques (such as strip cropping) in use at the time of the interview.[1] The regression results indicate that tenancy, if anything, may be conducive to better husbandry rather than exploitive use. It is also worth noting that a relatively high degree of ownership is associated with a lower volume of farm sales and greater reliance on off-farm income—the part-time farming syndrome. Whether this means that a high degree of ownership is associated with land of poorer quality and thus more need for erosion control was not demonstrated in this study, but may be worth investigating.

Closely related to the question of tenancy and its relationship to resource use is the question of landlord influence on farmer behavior as it may affect resource use. Dillman and Carlson (1982) suggest that landlords may be implicated in resource-conserving behavior in any of three ways. First, landlords may in essence prohibit the use of conservation practices on their land. Second, landlords may undo the actions of their tenants who opt for conservation practices by canceling their lease or rental agreement. And third, farm operators may find it convenient to "blame the landlord" for failing to adopt conservation practices when in fact the decision was their own.

Dillman and Carlson (1982) employed data from three surveys centered on a two-county area in the Palouse region of Washington. A sample of farmers in the area was surveyed in 1976 and contacted again in 1980. And a sample of absentee landlords, owning land in those counties but not living in the counties, was contacted in 1977. The upshot of Dillman and Carlson's (1982) analysis was that the first two possibilities mentioned above were not supported, but the possibility that landlords might serve as a convenient excuse for farmers' non-adoption of conservation practices could not be ruled out. Very few farmers in the sample actually cited their landlords as the most important obstacle to adoption, though substantially more mentioned the landlord as one of several obstacles. Landlords, on the other had, were more likely to perceive soil erosion as a problem than their farmer tenants thought was the case. In any case, for this sample, the idea that landlords might be an important factor contributing to exploitive land use was not supported.

Since a great deal of commercial farm land is operated by non-owners it seem likely that landlord influences on adoption decisions would merit more research attention in the future. The same would hold for managerial intermediaries between the landlord and the tenant, such as professional farm managers. Historically, diffusion researchers have assumed that the farm operator was not only the primary but the sole decision maker. Redefinitions of the approach to diffusion might well consider such "outside" influences as the landlord and landlord's managerial representatives.

Before leaving the discussion of capital intensity and related factors as possibly conducive to exploitive use of resources, I want to describe one study that deals with energy intensity. The worldwide increase in energy prices of the 1970s attracted considerable attention to energy usage and, among rural sociologists, the possible relationship between farm structure and energy intensity. Heaton and Brown's (1982) analysis of that issue can serve to summarize some of this work.

Heaton and Brown (1982) set out to expand upon some earlier studies that had supported the idea that scale of production is positively associated with energy intensity, at least in crop production (see, especially, Buttel and Larson, 1979). Heaton and Brown (1982) employed county-level rather than state-level data to assess the relationship between average farm size and county-level expenditures for energy in the form of fuel, fertilizer, and pesticides. They conclude (Heaton and Brown, 1982:27) that "counties with larger farms will generally spend less on energy per dollar value of product sold." Further, employing data from two points in time (1969 and 1974), Heaton and Brown (1982:27) conclude that "counties with larger farm units [tend] to have a lower rate of increase in energy use per dollar of sales than smaller farm counties and counties with growing farm size tend to experience a lower rate of growth in energy intensity than counties where farm size is not growing as rapidly." Mechanization, on the other hand, "seems to have a relatively separate effect on energy intensity from that of farm size" (Heaton and Brown, 1982:27).

In short, Heaton and Brown (1982) substantially challenge the idea that sheer farm size leads to greater energy usage, though capital intensity in the form of mechanization may do so. As is so often the case, global propositions don't hold up very well when confronted with data from a complex world. Among the complexities that Heaton and Brown (1982) as well as Buttel and Larson (1979) note is the matter of regional variability in farming conditions, addressed more directly in the following section.

Has ecological variability been adequately incorporated into diffusion theory? This third, and final, question that I have chosen as a device to summarize research on diffusion as related to environmental concerns has been answered in the negative in a number of recent research reports. Much of the material that I reviewed on control of soil erosion of course speaks to the question. Soil erosion and its on- and off-site effects are highly variable across locations. Ashby (1982), however, is among those who raise the question with respect to other types of technology as well.

Ashby (1982) utilizes data from three locations in Nepal that differ substantially in altitude. Diffusion rates for hybrid varieties of maize and rice are shown to differ in the three locations, and Ashby (1982) argues, with supporting data, that apparent differences in farmer innovativeness are at least partially a function of differences in both environmental and social-organizational characteristics of the three settings from which data were obtained.

The Nepalese study (Ashby, 1982) and a later study set in Colombia (Ashby, 1985) both raise questions about location-specific factors that may affect diffusion. In a sense the emphasis on location-specific variability reminds one of an earlier debate that, for example, cited variability in neighborhood norms (e.g., Marsh and Coleman, 1954, noted in Chapter 2) as a factor affecting diffusion rates. One underlying issue here is the still-to-be-resolved question as to whether innovativeness is a personality trait and, if so, whether it can be measured at an abstract level.

Ecological variability represents a recent addition to the debate, supplementing the focus on variations in norms, and a range of technical questions concerning specifications of the adoption decision. Ashby's (1982, 1985) focus on small farmers in third world settings fairly explicitly raises the equity issue also, however, by questioning the appropriateness of recommended agricultural technology not only to smallholders' ecological circumstances but to the social-organizational conditions under which smallholders operate.

I do not propose to delve into the literature on appropriate technology here. The literature is extensive and is not irrelevant to research on diffusion, but it ranges over much more than agriculture, and much of it is polemical in nature. I am sympathetic to Morrison's (1983) treatment of that literature via a "social movement" approach, but I doubt that I could tie that approach and the relevant literature back to rural sociologists' work in diffusion in an efficient manner. One of the more obvious points of intersection between diffusion research and the literature on appropriate technology is the smallholder equity issue Ashby (1982, 1985) raises. The question of inability to adopt, concerning which I cited Galjart's (1971) research on Brazilian smallholders in Chapter 3, can be turned around. It is of course theoretically possible to work toward designing technology that is optimal with respect to both the ecological and socioeconomic circumstances of the smallholder.

Research and development of location-specific technology is not a new issue, though how far such an emphasis can and should be pursued is not settled. The development of an array of International Agricultural Research Centers (IARCs) represents a major step in that direction. Ideally, the broad mandates of the IARCs are linked through national and sub-national agricultural research systems with the ultimate objective of designing technology well suited to particular local conditions. At this point in time there is still plenty of scope for further targeting of technology development efforts, though the political feasibility of directing such efforts to particular subsets of growers and growing conditions may well be an issue.

I agree with Ashby's (1985) call for a socioecological perspective in diffusion research. I can think of no better way to specify the question of "appropriate technology" in agriculture than to empirically assess the fit between available technology and both the physical and social conditions extant in particular settings. I also think that the research on diffusion done by geographers is relevant here, though largely ignored by rural sociologists. Brown et al. (1976) called for attention to the location and density of elements of the agricultural infrastructure by rural sociologists, but they don't seem to have had an impact. More broadly, of course, Brown's (1981) book-length treatment of diffusion doesn't seem to have penetrated the barrier between disciplines either. All of which is to say that there is room for expansion of the environmentally oriented work of rural sociologists on diffusion of innovations.[2]

MINING SOME OLD DIFFUSION DATA

Rural sociologists have historically relied on the sample survey to obtain data. Furthermore, the samples used to obtain data have tended to be relatively small and representative of relevant target populations in, say, one or two counties. Rural sociologists' professional orientation to problem solution can be cited as one reason for location-specific sampling, since a given problem may be perceived as more acute in some locations than in others. The relatively reliable but typically modest research funding available through agricultural experiment stations and similar organizations is probably the major reason for research based on small samples, however. While rural sociologists have frequently made efforts to compare sample characteristics with the characteristics of larger populations in an effort to enhance the generalizability of research results, the fact remains that the basis for knowledge of many rural phenomena consists of bits and pieces.

The proliferation of small-scale studies on diffusion of agricultural innovations provides a basis for the kind of meta-research that Rogers (1983:126-132) has undertaken with considerable success. Bits and pieces can be aggregated and in a determination can be made as to whether the evidence points in one direction or another. Rogers (1983:130-131) is quite willing to recognize that tabulating the results of many studies as either supporting or not supporting a two-variable proposition does not do justice to the complexities involved in human behavior. He also points out, in the same context, that much of the diffusion research literature is cast in precisely such two-variable terms.

Frank Cancian (1967) undertook a type of meta-research different from that described above by re-analyzing limited amounts of data from a variety of existing data sets and then essentially treating the newly determined results from each study as cases supporting or not supporting a broader proposition. Results were not simply accepted as published, in other words, but the underlying data were re-analyzed on the basis of a common set of concepts.

Cancian's (1967) initial study stimulated a sequence of further studies extended over two decades. The stimulating effect alone would make the work worthy of attention, but I want at least to mention two other points here. First, in spite of the increasing availability of sophisticated data-processing equipment it was, is, and will likely continue to be uncommon for researchers to re-analyze data from a range of studies. I suspect that the hard work involved in determining how a variety of conventions in the measurement, coding, and formatting of data might be deciphered and adjusted to a common framework is a major deterrent. And second, all good intentions to the contrary notwithstanding, it remains uncommon among rural sociologists to pose hypotheses in general terms and test them at that level. There is an inherent tension involved in doing applied research and also attempting to contribute to disciplinary knowledge, in my opinion. And my guess is that such tension inhibits efforts at either extreme. Whether the preferred middle ground is indeed a "happy medium" is not always obvious, but the immediate point is that attempts to establish truly general propositions are worth nothing simply because they are rare.

What Cancian (1967) did was to question the widely held but largely untested assumption that the relationship between farmers' socioeconomic status and readiness to adopt new technology is linear. Cancian (1967:913) put it as follows: "Though the association between wealth and early adoption is almost always found in empirical studies, the 'casual' relationship that is suggested seems…to be contrary to common first principles. Crudely stated, the argument might go as follows: The better your financial position, the more you have to lose and the less you have to gain from taking chances; therefore, insofar as adopting an innovation is risky, the richer you are, the less likely you are to adopt."

Put differently, the risk of loss in adopting a relatively unknown innovation should serve to inhibit adoption among those who have most to lose. Conversely, as more becomes known about the performance of an innovation, risk is reduced, and greater wealth should facilitate adoption. With the further proviso that extreme poverty may make any unacceptable and that extreme wealth may make such risk negligible, Cancian's (1967) argument combines the hypothesized inhibiting and facilitating effects to point toward an expected relationship such as that depicted in Figure 6. The focus in Figure 6 is on the risk of loss in status in the middle ranks and the expectation that this will be conducive to conservative behavior. I should point out that the form of the relationship depicted in Figure 6 is the expected form at an early stage in the diffusion process. At later stages the inhibiting effect of risk is expected to be less because more is known about a new technology, and the facilitating effect of wealth is expected to dominate.

I have left out many of the details of Cancian's (1967) argument in trying to present its central features. The argument was tested by re-analyzing data from seven existing diffusion studies, based on a total of 1624 cases from three countries. Cancian (1967:921) divided each of the seven samples into rank quartiles based on measures of farmer wealth available in the studies, most often the amount of land cultivated. He then separated out the highest quartile of adopters in each sample, those presumably facing most risk in adopting relatively unknown innovations, and determined whether the distribution of these early adopters across ranks conformed to the pattern illustrated in Figure 6. He concluded (Cancian, 1967:924) that the hypothesized pattern was in evidence for six of the seven samples analyzed. He also concluded that the hypothesized pattern, cited as evidence of upper-middle-class conservatism, was by and large not in evidence for respondents in the next lower ranking adoption quartile, that is, among respondents presumed to be facing less risk.

Figure 6
The Hypothesized Effect of Upper-Middle-Class Conservatism on the Relationship Between Economic Rank and Early Adoption of Agricultural Practices

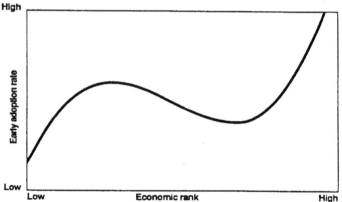

Note: From Gartrell and Gartrell (1985:39) and originally from Cancian (1979:3)

As Gartrell and Gartrell (1985:38) put it, "Cancian's contentions have elicited a flurry of theoretical and methodological criticism" over the years. I will not review that flurry here except to indicate that additional sample surveys were offered to further test the argument and that some of the measurement strategies were challenged. Cancian went to considerable lengths to incorporate additional samples and alternative theoretical formulations into his research design, most notably in a comprehensive monograph on the middle-class conservatism theme (Cancian, 1979). One of the extensions of the general argument treated at some length in the monograph is Cancian's insistence that status differences should be assessed in terms of the respondent's "community of reference" (Cancian, 1979:34-38; also Cancian, 1981). Loosely stated, the idea involved is that while global measures of status may have their value, it is the farmer's standing in some local community that is at risk in the adoption decision, and therefore it is location-specific rank that is critical in the research design. I take note of this point here because it seems to be consistent with a broader tendency in the research on diffusion to take location-specific variability into account.

The Gartrell and Gartrell (1985) study briefly mentioned above is, at this writing, the most recent analysis of the "Cancian dip" hypothesis in the literature. It takes into account the debates in the intervening years and also takes a significant step toward testing the hypothesis of a nonlinear relationship, as shown in Figure 6, in a generic manner. Briefly, what Gartrell and Gartrell (1985) did was to assess the relative strength of linear and non-linear (cubic) components in the status-innovation relationship for a total of thirty-four samples stemming from ten nations. It is not merely the existence of curvilinearity in a given relationship that is at issue, but the strength of the curvilinearity component. Gartrell and Gartrell (1985:48) draw the following conclusions: "Cancian's theory predicts the existence but not the magnitude of the cubic effect. Our results support his theory insofar as cubic effects exist; however, across studies and analyses, the status-innovation relationship appears to be linear, and Cancian's theory appears to have very small marginal utility in explaining innovation."

I doubt that the last word has been said or written about the linearity or non- linearity of the relationship between farmers' status and their propensity to adopt agricultural innovations. A tendency toward conservatism among middle-status farmers may be real but relatively unimportant, as Gartrell and Gartrell (1985) conclude. Since the status-innovation relationship is fundamental to the entire area of research, however, it seems likely that the nature of that relationship will receive additional research attention in the future. In the meantime, the subset of the diffusion literature that I have briefly touched on here can serve as a very positive example of the utility of moving beyond "narrative integration" of research results to "statistical integration" (Gartrell and Gartrell, 1985:39) and thereby achieving a more solid knowledge base.

DIFFUSION RESEARCH AND THE SYSTEMS PERSPECTIVE

In concluding this chapter on current research dealing with diffusion I want to take note of some changes in both the tactics and strategies employed to develop and transfer agricultural technology to farmers. On balance I will argue that these changes shift attention away from both the "classic" approach to diffusion via communication and the structural approaches emphasized recently. Whether research on diffusion of innovations will be substantially affected in the long run is an open question, in my opinion.

Some of the early diffusion studies focused on single innovations, such as hybrid corn. The pattern that soon emerged, however, stressed composite measures, intended to specify individual innovativeness as a personality trait. By and large the composite measures assumed that one innovation was like another for measurement purposes. The preference for composite measures was challenged from time to time by efforts to isolate distinctive types of technology, a recent example of which is the distinction between production enhancing and conservation technology, discussed earlier in this chapter. Isolating subsets of innovations on the basis of particular attributes such as their potential profitability is another example of the challenge to treating each innovation like every other for measurement purposes. The classification of agricultural innovations, in general, into presumably more homogeneous subsets has still meant that innovations within subsets were treated as equivalent for measurement purposes.

Diffusion researchers have not formally dealt with the fact that the combined effect of adopting, say, a new seed variety *and* fertilizer applied to that variety has a significance beyond the adoption of two randomly selected innovations. The effects of some innovations are enhanced *if* certain other innovations are also adopted, which is to say that two or more apparently dissimilar innovation may, in combination, have an impact that is more than the sum of individual effects. Measures of innovativeness have not considered the possibility or even the demonstrated probability that the effects of adoption involve interaction among innovations.[3]

It may be simplistic to argue that, as improved agricultural technology accumulated, the tactics involved in dissemination have shifted from advocacy of single innovations to advocacy of subsets in "packages" of technology. Whatever the causes of a shift, it is a fact that increased emphasis on combinations or packages of technology has been evident of several decades. One of the more obvious examples of that kind of emphasis is the provision of "in kind" production credit in the form of seed-fertilizer packages, which is fairly common in third-world, smallholder credit programs. Another example is the practice of specifying an array of inputs to be used by those who farm under contract with some off-farm entity. At a much more general level, however, diffusion strategies have increasingly emphasized combinations of technologies in order to realize the joint effects demonstrated in experimental situations but frequently not realized in on-farm applications.

Technology development also seems to have shifted more toward multi-item or multi-activity packages to deal with problems faced in the production process. I regard integrated pest management as a good example of the increasing complexity of recent technology development efforts. Integrated pest management involves detailed monitoring of pest problems and selective application of pest control measures at a point where prospects for pest damage are judged to justify application of some control measure. A key idea is the tolerance of minor pest damage and limited utilization of particular control measures that put a ceiling on pest damage but do not necessarily eliminate a particular pest. Integrated pest management thus involves a set of practices called into play depending on location-specific conditions. The choice of practices can be expected to vary from location to location and thus it becomes difficult to specify "the" innovation and at what point the innovative act has taken place. If pest invasions are minimal then presumably no action beyond monitoring would be called for.

My general point here is that there is a substantial difference between specifying an act of adoption and the ultimate diffusion of an innovation which has a distinctive and concrete manifestation, say hybrid corn, and applying the same research techniques to a congeries of innovations designed for selective use in order to achieve an optimal solution to a particular problem. Precisely what is being diffused, when, and for what reasons is hard to pin down when the objective is to maximize efficiency rather than achieve adoption of a concrete entity without considering other innovations or traditional practices at the same time.

The heading that I chose for this section of the chapter on current diffusion efforts is "Diffusion Research and the Systems Perspective." I used the word "systems" with some trepidation because it means different things to different people. I have tried to cite examples of what I view as a trend in both the development and transfer of agricultural technology. This is a trend toward the design and advocacy of "packages" of technology intended for joint use, and toward clusters of alternative practices from which a given farmer makes a selection depending on circumstances at a certain place and time. Thus far I have chosen to use words like package and cluster to designate increasingly complex combinations of technologies in order to avoid some of the more formal connotations of the term "systems." The general notion of combinations of elements and interdependencies is there, however, and in recent years that type of notion, or idea, has been broadened to include the farmer and farm situation. Thus we now hear about the design of technology systems and about farming systems in a more formal sense.

The development of the mechanical tomato harvester is described by Schmitz and Seckler (1984:105) as an example of the systems approach to technology development. Mechanical harvesting equipment was designed, but plant material that would lend themselves to mechanical harvesting were designed as well. Tomato processors were involved in the research and development work also in order to smooth the transition to a new production system. And finally, growers were involved in the research on and development of the new system.

Grower involvement in the development of the mechanical tomato harvester is the nub of some of the controversy about the new system (Schmitz and Seckler, 1984). Hand labor was displaced by the new machine-based system and the issue of equity in sharing the benefits of the new system has been the subject of considerable controversy. I will not dwell on that controversy but will bring to a close my discussion of "the case of the tomato harvester" by making two points. My first and main point is that grower involvement in the technology development process makes it difficult to specify an adoption decision. The farmer's decision does not follow *after* the design and introduction of a technology but is part of the process itself. Rural sociologists' preference for survey methods and attempts to specify and explain adoption decisions, singly or via composite measures, do not lend themselves well to analyses of phenomena such as the introduction of the new tomato production system. And my second point is that I see no inherent difference between the research and development process I have described above and the farming systems approach that has recently become popular, especially in developing countries.[4] It is not clear to me that rural sociologists' commonly used research techniques are very useful in the systems approach to technology development and transfer, and that may have an impact on diffusion research in the future.

A recent discussion of research on adoption from the perspective of economics makes the following suggestion: "A complete analytical perspective for investigating adoption processes at the farm level should include a model of the farmer's decision making about the extent and intensity of use of the new technology at each point throughout the adoption process and a set of equations of motion describing the time pattern of parameters that affect the farmer's decision" (Feder et al., 1985:257). Considerably more detailed measurement and also more sophisticated analytic techniques, in other words, may aid in analyses of complex adoption decision. Or, if one doesn't care to borrow from economics, the methods of anthropology present another alternative. Rhodes (1984:17-38) provides an interesting example of anthropologists' work on designing post-harvest technology for Peruvian potato farmers by bringing the farmers' perspective to bear on the design process. The latter is an example of interdisciplinary work from the farming systems perspective. At the outset the emphasis is put on technology design but the intent of course is to achieve diffusion through appropriate design. Analyses of diffusion from the farming systems perspective are not yet visible in the rural sociological literature.

I am unable to predict whether rural sociologists' research on the diffusion of complex technology packages or diffusion via the farming systems approach to introducing technology will be much affected by greater emphasis on either quantitative or qualitative methods. I am persuaded that the methods in current use, and the conceptual approaches behind those methods, are of limited use. Some changes may be forthcoming, but such changes may mean that the initiative for doing diffusion research will come from different disciplines in the future.

CONCLUSIONS

In this chapter I reviewed the research on diffusion of innovations that rural sociologists have undertaken recently. I devoted most attention to research on the diffusion of resource-conserving technology because it seemed to me that rural sociologists have concentrated on this area recently. There is a considerable amount of continuity evident when one compares the recent research with that of the past. The structural antecedents of adoption – farm size, farm tenure, education – clearly receive more attention than the farmer's beliefs, attitudes, or communication behavior. Similarly, equity concerns are basic to the work in the resource-conservation area, though intergenerational equity and individual/societal equity questions are more prominent than the inter-individual concerns that I discussed in the preceding chapter.

By and large the research on diffusion of resource-conserving technology has built on an older pattern that stressed structural concerns and a relatively macroscopic view of diffusion phenomena. At the same time, however, the emphasis in this work on ecological variability, and the fit between different kinds of conservation technology and such site-specific variability, has reintroduced a microanalytic perspective in a different form.

In the middle section of the chapter I discussed a somewhat different subset of diffusion studies, one that capitalized on past studies in order to arrive at universalistic propositions about the relationship between the farm operator's structural position and adoption behavior. Here again there is continuity in the emphasis on social structure, and of course the quest for generally valid propositions is macroscopic by definition. But here also a microscopic element is retained in the emphasis on assessing the research subject's status position in terms of the community of reference.

Finally, in the last section of the chapter, I addressed what I see as a rather uneasy tension between micro- and macro-perspectives in a more explicit manner. There I briefly discussed the contemporary emphasis on packages of technology, from the simple combining of elements of existing technology to the deliberate design of production systems, including site-specific design as is emphasized in farming systems research. I argued that the standard research techniques in use by rural sociologists are not well suited to discerning what innovation is being adopted when and for what reason when variable combinations of technologies are tailored to particular circumstances.

It is not obvious to me how one can generalize about diffusion, that is take a macroscopic perspective, when what is being diffused is variable. One alternative would be to focus on effects rather than adoption, as is at least implicitly the case in the Heffernan and Green (1986) work on soil conservation technologies in which they designated estimated soil loss as the variable of interest. And other approaches, as I indicated in the preceding section, are to shift more heavily toward complex, econometric designs or employ case study and ethnographic methods.

The next, and final, chapter is intended to be more futuristic in orientation. There, with the help of a crystal ball, I will try to provide a more clear and balanced view of the future directions of diffusion research.

NOTES

1. Discussion of the adoption of farm financial practices, also analyzed by Albrecht and Thomas (1986) with the result shown in Table 7, does not fit as part of the soil conservation theme here. I don't wish to ignore it entirely, however, because innovations in this area (e.g., forward contracting and cash flow statement) are of increasing importance to commercial agriculture and have thus far been virtually ignored in research on diffusion. Financial management tools may be at least as important to the future of agriculture as, say, tillage equipment.

2. Another interesting possibility for further development of an ecological perspective may lie in the ecological-evolutionary theory of Lenski and Nolan (1984) and Nolan and Lenski (1985). These authors draw attention to the heritage of agricultural technology that developing societies bring to the development process and attempt to trace the influence of differences in such heritages on the development trajectories of such societies. Their approach might be useful with respect to agricultural development as well.

3. Some of the environmentally oriented diffusion research indicates a sensitivity to this issue, but I am not aware that adoption measures which take interaction into account have been devised. Heffernan and Green (1986), for example, use "estimated soil loss," an outcome variable, in their analysis. One could view such a measure as a surrogate for adoption of conservation practices, though it would require something of a leap of faith.

4. Much of the farming systems work has been oriented to smallholder agriculture, in part to redress equity problems. In that sense, the tomato harvester example differs from what is usually treated under the farming systems label.

6

Prospects for the Future

In the several chapters of this monograph I have tried to sketch out the early efforts of rural sociologists to do research on diffusion of agricultural innovations, how and why an essentially behaviorist approach became the norm for such research, and how that approach was gradually modified over time. All of that review was sketchy. I'd like to say that the sketchiness was necessary in view of space limitations, but I preferred that path in any case. I chose to emphasize some of the twists and turns in a long span of research activity in order to provide a few anchoring points to aid a serious scholar in comprehending a substantial body of research literature.

I ended the preceding chapter, dealing with recent research, on a rather pessimistic note. There I argued that the increasing complexity of agricultural technology and the recent emphasis on design of entire production systems might call for research methods not now in common use among rural sociologists and thus escape from the research nets rural sociologists cast. In this final chapter I want to first back off that pessimistic note and take a broader look at the technological change process on a global scale. Following that, I want to briefly recapitulate what I see as the major conceptual shifts that have characterized the work on diffusion and assess the present situation from a conceptual perspective. Then, finally, I will devote the balance of the chapter to what may occur in the future. Crystal balls tend to be murky, and probably reflect only what one would like to see or has the capacity to see. If that is the case I will probably only be stating some personal preferences, also known as biases.

A GLOBAL PERSPECTIVE ON CURRENT DIFFUSION PHENOMENA

I do, in fact, believe that an emphasis on the interdependencies among the many elements involved in the food and fiber production process is the wave of the future. I take that position because agricultural production has gradually become a science-based process and because scientific knowledge, for better or worse, is cumulative. The knowledge base for refining the production process is broadening over time, and that base in itself provides options for further rationalization of the actual production process. That view has to be tempered, however, by taking into account several other facts. First, the technological change process in agriculture is a long-term phenomenon. One tends to forget that the diffusion of hybrid corn in the U.S. cornbelt extended over a full generation. There are instances of much more rapid diffusion such as the rapid spread of short-stemmed wheat varieties in parts of Asia, but by and large the diffusion of innovations is a long-term process. Second, one must keep in mind that the global transformation of agriculture is very uneven. I touched on that point in the discussion of equity issues in Chapter 4. But apart from possible local and regional inequities in the impacts of technological change, one must recognize that substantial parts of Africa, for example, are as yet essentially unaffected by modern agricultural technology.

Any transformation of agriculture in settings as yet largely unaffected by modern technology will probably be both gradual and piece-meal. I am confident that there will continue to be a high level of interest in speeding up the diffusion of relatively simple as well as complex technologies in many parts of the world, and thus considerable demand for much the same kind of diffusion research that has been done in the past. Some of that research may well be more immediately useful for planning local action programs than in contributing to a fund of scientific knowledge. That should not detract from the value of such work, however. In my opinion, highly applied work only loses value when the researcher him- or herself strains to dress up such work as a contribution to knowledge, with a capital K, and thus fails to exploit the practical value.

I wish to make a further point in this section, and that is that some quite "conventional" diffusion research can be futuristic in orientation and also contribute to knowledge. The current work on diffusion of conservation technology is of course an example of that. I want to describe an example from the third world, however, to offset the possible inference that I am advocating the export and recycling of outdated research procedures to countries dependent on the larges of what are known as donor nations.

Prospects For the Future

The example I wish to describe features an experimental design in which instructional materials were conveyed via satellite to audiences in Indian villages provided with television receivers (Shingi et al., 1982). The purpose of the experiment was to determine whether such methods could be used to reduce the gap in knowledge about modern agriculture between those farmers usually not reached by other methods and those who had better access to information sources. Shingi et al. (1982:6) were unable to gather benchmark data prior to initiation of the adult education campaign. They thus used a split-sample design with non-viewers of the program series as the control group. Their detailed analysis demonstrated that farm operators who viewed the specially designed programs on the modernization of agriculture retained knowledge of program content, and that knowledge levels did not vary by socioeconomic status (Shingi et al., 1982:117). The hypothesis that mass media introduction would widen the gap in knowledge between rich and poor, as earlier proposed by Tichenor (1970), was not supported. The key, of course, was the intervention from outside the system that made television receivers available at the village level and made instructional programs accessible to both rich and poor.

One reason for singling out the Shingi et al. (1982) report of an experiment with instruction via satellite and television is that it emphasizes a highly sophisticated and futuristic technology put to use in a third world setting. In addition, the work is also future-oriented in that is assesses a means of intervention intended to bring about change. Most research on diffusion attempts to reconstruct the past, but with an eye toward ways of intervening to overcome restraints on adoption. Experimental designs can directly assess the feasibility of such intervention and in that sense are more explicitly future-oriented.

Another reason for describing the television experiment above is that it reminds me of Hoffer's (1942) experiment to test the effectiveness of different print materials in reaching Michigan celery growers, a study I cited as one of the earliest in the diffusion research tradition. It is probably coincidental that Shingi et al. (1982) also used an experimental design. I do not think that it is coincidental that both dealt with communication techniques. The recent de-emphasis of a communications approach in favor of a structural approach to diffusion of agricultural technology should not be interpreted to mean that information and knowledge transfer are unimportant in understanding the diffusion process. Both approaches are useful, and of course the television experiment illustrates the importance of social structure as well as communication in its emphasis on reaching the poor as well as the rich farmers.

In summary, the technological revolution in agriculture is an ongoing process and an uneven process that takes different forms, depending on local needs and conditions. Contributions to understanding that process will continue to be in demand and will probably draw on a range of perspectives, again depending on local needs and conditions. No single model is likely to be applicable universally.

CONCEPTUAL SHIFTS IN DIFFUSION RESEARCH

Having already argued for the continuing viability of a communications approach to diffusion, above, I want to briefly recapitulate the conceptual shifts that have taken place in this research area and assess the current situation. I have repeatedly stated that the early diffusion studies were socio-psychological in their approach. The farm operator was viewed as an actor, in a given situation, influenced by certain structural constraints and by certain social and cultural circumstances to behave in a predictable way. The research objective was to understand the reason for the farmer's behavior and work toward altering those limiting factors that could be manipulated most easily. Given the twin assumptions that agricultural technology was beneficial to the farmer and that the farmer was free to choose for or against adoption, researchers tended to focus on access to knowledge about technology as the area in which manipulation of the diffusion process would be most useful.

With the transfer of what came to be called the "classic" diffusion model to third world settings it was gradually realized that the earlier assumption that the farm operator was free to choose for or against adoption was questionable. Farmers with extremely limited resources could not be viewed as free to act, and manipulating information flows would therefore not be effective. Attention thus shifted to ways of ameliorating the limiting effects of resource constraints, or more bluntly stated, poverty, and in some situations attention shifted to altering the social structure itself. In a sense, blaming the structure replaced the victim-blaming emphasis that was said to characterize the "classic" approach.

Questions about the assumption that farmers were free to act were closely associated with questions about the assumed benefits of agricultural technology. Diffusion researchers shifted from assuming that the benefits of agricultural technology were obvious to asking questions about benefit to whom. In my opinion, a tendency to blame the structure, and at times even to blame the technology itself, for differences in the benefits of technology accruing to farmers has inhibited research on the general issue among sociologists. In any case, much work remains to be done.

Questions about the benefits of technology stem from another source as well. The unintended environmental consequences of technological change have attracted research attention, as was detailed in Chapter 5. Both sources of questions about the benefits of agricultural technology have contributed to a tendency among diffusion researchers to shift away from treating innovativeness as a general personality trait. A focus on particular types of technology rather than technology in general is of course not new in diffusion research. That issue has come up in several of the preceding chapters. Another non-novelty, however, is the continued emphasis on innovativeness as a personal trait, albeit only a certain kind of innovativeness. The unit of analysis has been the individual throughout the history of diffusion research, though the quest for explanatory factors has shifted toward measures of the individual's position in the social structure.

Diffusion research has by no means been atheoretical, but it has never been theory driven. The approach has been to draw on at least middle-range propositions about human behavior to decode what has happened, retrospectively, in a given diffusion situation. Throughout, the driving force has been practical, to find levers that would make the diffusion process more rapid or more efficient in reaching certain target categories of farmers. The approach has therefore been substantially inductive, reasoning from what is to what might be.[1]

The quest for means of intervening in the diffusion process is related to the fact that, historically, much of the technology of concern had its origin in public sector research institutions. Mechanical innovations are the major exception. Obvious clients for knowledge about manipulating the diffusion process were therefore the people responsible for technology transfer in those same institutions. This situation is changing, however, and it is not clear how some of the more future-oriented diffusion research will relate to the emerging technology generation establishment (Ruttan, 1982).

Mechanical technology has had its origins in the private sector, for the most part, largely because research and development costs could be recaptured by way of patents on the product. The gradual emergence of patent or patent-like protection for plant and animal technologies is changing that situation. How far the shift of both the more applied aspects of technology generation as well as technology transfer will go away from the public sector and into the private sector is impossible to say. But the shift is taking place now and it will have implications for rural sociologists' research on diffusion. One alternative is to shift the work (even) more toward a marketing perspective, with emphasis on manipulating the subject. Another alternative is to focus on those technologies most likely to remain under the control of the public sector, such as resource-conserving technologies.

Still another alternative is to focus on the possibilities for control of the diffusion process by doing *ex ante* rather than *ex post* studies. The *ex ante* designs are used essentially to forecast the impact or consequences of an innovation. Rossi et al. (1979:242) define *ex ante* designs (in the context of cost-efficiency or cost-benefit analyses) as analyses "undertaken prior to program implementation to estimate net outcome in relation to costs." In the context of diffusion, *ex ante* analyses would be undertaken prior to the adoption of a technology in order to estimate outcomes and costs. Analyses would be based on assumptions and estimates made from previous research in the area or in related areas.

The *ex post* studies, undertaken after one knows the outcomes and effects, are especially valuable for subsequent policy planning and decision-making. This alternative is particularly attractive and well-suited for the analysis of the "revolutionary" technologies on the horizon.

Although the methods and current conceptual approach to diffusion are not well suited to *ex ante* studies, a few researchers have incorporated such designs in their studies. Others have used *ex post* designs and I will expand on these examples in the following section.

THE TECHNOLOGY OF THE FUTURE AND DIFFUSION RESEARCH

The popular press as well as scholarly journals make reference to "revolutionary" new agricultural technologies with some frequency at present. Part of the reason for what may well be no more than hyperbole could be the situation of relative abundance of agricultural production and correspondingly low commodity prices of the mid-1980s. A revolution can provide hope in a time of crisis. Another and more fundamental reason for talk of revolution, however, is the fact of a cumulative knowledge base in science. Some of the current research and development activity that capitalizes on that base shows great promise.

I am referring here, of course, to current activity in areas of biotechnology and electronics. Buttel at al. (1985) focus on what they call the "biorevolution." Lasley and Bultena (1986) talk about "third-wave" technologies, and Tweeten (1986) describes the current situation in U.S. agriculture as somewhere between the third and fourth technological "revolution." These examples should suffice to document the point that there is indeed interest in some new developments in agricultural technology and an expectation that such technologies could make a radical difference in agriculture.

Although I am quite willing to apply the term "revolution" to the aggregate transformation of the agricultural production process that has been under way for at least decades, I have reservations about using the term for subsets of the larger aggregate. I agree with Buttel et al. (1985) that biotechnology may have more pervasive impacts than the so-called green revolution. The latter term is usually applied to developments in seed-fertilizer technology while the emerging possibilities in biotechnology have implications for many aspects of both plant and animal agriculture. Yet I am also aware that the talk of a revolution colored green was shortly followed by assertions that the revolution had failed. No miraculous cure for the world's food problem had been found. None should have been expected.

I doubt that there is a technological fix in the offing for the problems of the 1980s for three main reasons. First and foremost, one should be hesitant about treating possibilities as probabilities, and the current discussion is clearly about what may occur in the future. Science does not guarantee specific results. Second, with reference to biotechnology, there is a great deal of uncertainty at present about

97

regulations to protect the public from unknown hazards that the release of new technologies into the environment might bring about. It is clear that the field testing and eventual release of many new biotechnologies is not to be taken for granted.[2] And third, with reference to computer-telecommunications technologies, there is reason to think that the most substantial implications of the new technologies will apply to large-scale agriculture only. In short, I am arguing for caution in forecasting change. That is not to deny that some important possibilities for technological changes are on the horizon and that these possibilities will challenge rural sociologists.

A cotton management expert system known as Comax (Lemmon, 1986) can serve as an example of emerging technologies that centrally involve electronics. Comax was tested and refined on fifteen cotton farms in five state in 1986 and is moving toward wider application (Lemmon, 1986:33). Its developers make no claim for its eventual utility on other than farms with, say, 1,000 acres or more in cotton (Lemmon, 1986:33). Without going into detail on precisely what Comax is and does, it can be described as a computer model that simulates plant growth. That model is integrated with an expert system designed to determine the best strategies for fertilizing, irrigating, and so on (Lemmon, 1986:29). It relies on a large base of stored data supplemented by, for example, current weather information, with the intent of replacing management "rules of thumb" with science-based decision criteria. Early reports on the performance of the system are quite optimistic with respect to increasing yields and reducing production costs (Comis, 1986).

Comax is another example of interdisciplinary work that combines both public and private resources and relies on grower collaboration in order to design and develop a complex crop production system. Why should it be of interest to rural sociologists? At present adoption is not the issue; the technology is still under development. Given the backlog of research on technological change in rural sociology, one could expect some interest in a potentially important technological development in any case, and the possibility of anticipating change rather than studying such change in retrospect should be of interest.

One approach to research on the diffusion of computer technology is suggested by Audirac and Beaulieu (1986). It is not clearly an *ex ante* approach and is developed in the context of diffusion of microcomputers. They argue that the conditions for effective on-farm use of microcomputer capabilities cannot be taken for granted at the present. Against that background they suggest that Brown's (1981) approach to diffusion, which stresses the location and density of institutions that supply and service a given technology, may be more fruitful than some variant of the more familiar diffusion model. Put differently, they suggest that access to a service and support system may be a major determinant of eventual adoption. I think that the idea has merit and may be useful in analyses dealing with some of the less radically new biological innovations (e.g., the transplanting of embryos in animal agriculture) as well as management tools.

It is my guess that farmer access to services and support institutions should receive more attention in diffusion research. As increasingly complex technologies become available for farm use the traditional image of the farmer as "jack of all trades" becomes more a matter of wishful thinking than reality. I should go on to say that the same idea is relevant to the diffusion of simple technologies also. I am aware of some efforts to design quite simple mechanical devices for use in third world agriculture that more or less died stillborn for lack of locally available support services, for example, welding services for repair.

I believe that the geographer's emphasis on the spatial distribution and density of an array of support services (Brown, 1981) deserves more attention than it has received thus far. On the other hand, I see no inherent reason why relatively standard rural sociological research procedures cannot serve much the same purpose. In a recent paper a co-author and I (Fliegel and Tourinho, 1985) suggested the construction of dual measures of innovativeness. The first was a conventional measure of adoption of production technology. The second was a measure of adoption or utilization of "institutional technology." I would not argue for the use of a particular label, but the idea was to assess the respondent's innovativeness with respect to use of technical advisory services, financial services, marketing services, and so on. Whether one attempts to measure innovativeness with respect to services or treats that type of phenomenon as "access conditions to adoption," as Audirac and Beaulieu (1986:64) suggest, is less important than is the recognition that support services are important to the diffusion process. And, to repeat, as increasingly complex technologies become available to agriculture the role of support services increases in importance.

Returning to the previous discussion of Comax for a moment, I do *not* think that the kind of approach I have sketched out above will be useful in such a context. Comax is an example of a highly complex bundle of technologies being developed in conjunction with growers. The distinction between development and adoption is thus substantially blurred. It is not only complex also capital intensive and thus the number of potential adopters is quite limited. If development is successful, adoption is not much of an issue. It is the potential impact of such a technology that deserves attention. If Comax lives up to its promise – and this is certainly not guaranteed – what happens to small and medium-sized growers? Although Comax may apply to large farms, the basic idea of expert systems could be applicable without size constraints.

The kinds of *ex ante* and policy relevant studies that Berardi (1981) calls for would seem to be most useful here.[3] The few examples that Berardi (1981:491-493) was able to cite, tobacco harvesting and California vegetable studies, provide some guidelines. Berardi (1981) discusses this type of design as a means to evaluate the socioeconomic consequences of the adoption of a technology (in the tobacco industry) before it is widely diffused. Doing so would allow well-planned and well-executed adjustment and compensation programs to be put in place for those negatively affected by the technology transfer.

Johnson and Zahara (1976) used this design to examine critically technological research to anticipate potential efficiency and equity problems that may arise with the introduction of new technology, that is mechanization of harvesting iceberg lettuce. Friedland et al. (1981) used a projective design to examine the consequences of technological change in the lettuce industry. Even these few studies have not been dominated by rural sociologists, however, and I think the main reason for that lack of prominence can be traced to the choice of research methods. The dominant sample-survey and regression analysis procedures do not lend themselves to *ex ante* research, in my opinion.

Another approach to research on the diffusion of electronic technology is, of course, the approach I just rejected above, the sample-survey and regression approach. I will illustrate one application of that approach that attempts to predict what may happen and give some reasons for my doubtful posture. Lasley and Bultena's (1986) research on "third-wave" technologies includes but goes well beyond electronic technologies and relies on farmers' opinions about particular technologies to predict future action. These authors conclude that indexes of farmers' opinions about futuristic technology are not well predicted by a diffusion model that employs an array of fairly standard indicators of the farmers' socioeconomic status (Lasley and Bultena, 1986:125).

I agree with Lasley and Bultena's (1986) conclusion that a conventional diffusion approach will not be very useful in predicting adoption at some future point in time. I would not have expected such predictive power either, however. The technologies of the future are still rather vague shapes on the horizon. It is not clear to me that farmers' opinions about "genetic engineering research on plants," for example (Lasley and Bultena, 1986:124), should be expected to predict farmers' future adoption of some particular technology derived from that research. And even where technologies can be more clearly specified (e.g., personal computers for farm use, Lasley and Bultena, 1986:124), there are substantial grounds for doubting the utility of using current opinions to predict future behavior. There is a substantial literature on the latter subject that I won't go into here.

While I have doubts about some parts of Lasley and Bultena's (1986) approach, I will go on to say that current assessments of opinions and attitudes are by no means useless. I simply question whether an opinion or attitude measure can serve as a surrogate for a measure of future adoption behavior. At a more general level, I doubt that conventional measurement procedures can give reliable estimates of parameters at some future time. Thus I am inclined to think that a more nearly qualitative approach, a case study approach such as that used by Fredericks (1984) in analyzing technological change in the lettuce industry, will be more useful for discerning future trends.

Bovine growth hormone can serve as an example of biotechnology to complement the discussion of electronic technologies above. Bovine growth hormone is not new in one sense. It has long been known that "injection of a crude extract of bovine pituitary gland could boost a cow's milk output" (Sun, 1986:150). What is new is that modern bio-engineering techniques can make the refined product available for mass distribution. The product has not yet been approved for release and in that respect it typifies a problem faced by biotechnologies and differentiates them from electronic technologies. Also, unlike electronic technologies the bovine growth hormone is expected to directly increase production, and much of the controversy surrounding its approval for release stems directly from concern about production increases in the face of surplus production and weakness in prices.

Other similarities and differences between electronic and biotechnologies could be pointed out, but my immediate objective is to focus on an apparent similarity between technologies such as Comax and bovine growth hormone. Both have "revolutionary" overtones in that they are perceived as showing great promise. I do not believe that research on adoption and diffusion should be of major interest to sociologists for either technology. The impact of such technologies is problematic, and therefore *ex ante* studies that can assess possible impacts would seem to be most appropriate. Both cotton and milk are commodities in long supply. A technological change that can significantly increase production on the one hand or indirectly increase profit margins on the other can be expected to alter the competitive position of producers. Unlike Comax, there is no immediate reason to expect that small-scale dairy farmers could not adopt the hormone since no substantial capital investment is required. On the other hand, increased production per cow with accompanying changes in animal feeding practices and health care make heavy demands on managerial skills and small producers may well be disadvantaged in that respect (Sun, 1986:151). In short, a structural impact is not unlikely, and therefore some forecasting of possible impact should have high priority.

CONCLUSION

I have tried to give this chapter a "something old, something new" flavor. My rationale for taking that approach is that, from a global perspective, the technological transformation of agriculture is very uneven. Expert systems and complex biotechnologies are the wave of the future, though not all of these technologies have revolutionary overtones. But there are parts of the world where introducing animals as a source of energy to partially replace human energy in crop cultivation may be a preferred option for the foreseeable future (Ward et al., 1980).

Diffusion research was historically based on the practical motivation to smooth the flow of known technology to those who could put it to use. Perspectives on the constraints to using improved technology have broadened considerably over the years, but the practical motivation remains unchanged. While I do not regard the technological transformation of agriculture as inevitably headed in some particular direction, I do not think that it is realistic to assume that the transformation process can be somehow halted or even reversed. Thus I expect there to be a continuing need for efforts to understand particular aspects of the change process, work toward alleviating constraints to use of available technology, and efforts to ameliorate undesirable impacts. Rural sociologists have a role to play in meeting those continuing needs, a role limited only by our own ingenuity or lack of ingenuity.

NOTES

1. It seems to me plausible to argue that the focus on the individual farmer, and ways of influencing that farmer, explain why the induced innovation theory (Hayami and Ruttan, 1971) has had little impact on rural sociology. This theory, which relies on relative prices of the major factors of production to account for technology flows, is closer to a general theory of technological change in agriculture than anything I know of in sociology. It is probably more appropriate for explaining long-run, aggregate patterns of change than for analysis of individual behavior (deJanvry and Dethier, 1985:5-7), thus the lack of impact on rural sociology. Another explanation for the lack of impact, of course, is that sociologists and economists don't talk to each other.

2. A recent article in the popular press appeared under the headline, "Biotech's Stalled Revolution" (Schneider, 1986). The story dealt with the rapid rise and at least temporary halt in a major chemical company's effort to develop and field test a genetically altered microbial pesticide. Whether the present impasse regarding regulations for field testing genetically altered materials will result in a long-run disincentive for research in this area, especially private sector research, remains to be seen.

3. If Comax is successfully developed, I see no inherent reason why similar systems could not be developed for other commodities. In that case one could draw on inferences from the experience with one commodity to others and the forecasting task becomes somewhat more manageable.

Prospects For the Future

7

Diffusion Research in the 1990s and Beyond
Peter F. Korsching

In an article published in 1996 Vernon Ruttan, an agricultural economist, states that diffusion of innovations research has almost disappeared from the rural sociology research agenda. A similar observation was made by Rogers in the fourth edition (1995) of *Diffusion of Innovations*. Rogers states that since the late 1970s only a few diffusion-related publications written by rural sociologists have appeared. Rogers argues that the decline in attention by rural sociologists to the diffusion of innovations stems from the major theoretical and methodological issues of the model having been resolved. Although the model came under severe criticism in the late 1960s and 1970s, Rogers (1995) states that the decline is not a result of the criticism, rather the attraction of a dominant intellectual paradigm becoming exhausted. "The paradigm was not found inadequate in its explanatory power but rather it became stale as the main research questions were answered" (Rogers, 1995:60).

Ruttan's (1996) own perspective on this decline is that rural sociologists were too parochial in their outlook and approach to diffusion research. The convergence among research traditions for which there seemed such strong potential as diffusion research diffused to other disciplines in the 1960s never materialized. Rural sociologists have been little influenced by research in other disciplines. "… sociologists failed to embrace the more formal analytical methods introduced by the geographers to understand the process of spatial diffusion or by the economists and technologists to understand the process of technological innovation, substitution and replacement" (Ruttan, 1996:66). Indeed, when I teach the graduate level diffusion of innovations course, I use several chapters from Lawrence Brown's *Innovation Diffusion* (1981). Although the volume is now severely dated, it provides valuable insights into the overall innovation creation, development, promotion, diffusion, reinvention and impact processes. Rogers concurs on the importance of these topics by giving increasing attention to them in the newer editions of his book. Brown's (1981) insights are especially useful in the strategies for promoting innovations and, a topic on which diffusion research received much criticism, especially in its application in less developed countries, the necessity of the infrastructure and the problem of structural constraints for the diffusion of innovations.

Fliegel[1] also had some thoughts on the decline of diffusion research in rural sociology. In chapter six of this volume he touches upon issues raised by Rogers (1995) and Ruttan (1996), but adds that the dominant research methods of the field, survey research, do not lend themselves to a deeper understanding of the nuances of the diffusion process. Especially prominent by their absence are *ex ante* studies that may be useful in predicting future adoption of technologies. He states (p. 101) "... I doubt that conventional measurement procedures can give reliable estimates of parameters at some future time. Thus I am inclined to think that a more nearly qualitative approach ... will be more useful for discerning future trends." Fliegel also is somewhat critical of the tendency to blame the structure or the innovation itself for differences in the benefits of the innovation that accrued to various groups of farmers. Although this criticism was a reaction that came with the realization that farmers were not always free to act, it also has served to inhibit research.

Research on the diffusion of innovations has declined in rural sociology, but it has not vanished. In preparation for teaching the diffusion of innovations course I conduct a thorough review of journals that might contain articles on diffusion by rural sociologists, sociologists in general, and social scientists closely related to sociology. This literature search usually yields half-a-dozen new articles, and that number could even be higher depending on how loosely I define adoption and diffusion of innovations and closely related social sciences. As an indicator that this area of scholarship is not dead among sociologists and that new theoretical and methodological issues are being pursued, the November 1999 issue of the *Annals of the American Academy of Political and Social Science* had the topical theme "The Social Diffusion of Ideas and Things." Several of the articles were authored by sociologists. Also, diffusion studies often are cited in non-diffusion literature, usually in support of a discussion of some aspect of social change or development.

Granted, there is not synergy of a large number of rural sociologists and sociologists working collaboratively and competitively to advance the knowledge of this field. The "invisible college" that existed around this paradigm in the 1950s and 1960s (Rogers, 1995) probably is not even an invisible department at this point. When one scans the bibliographies of articles on diffusion of innovations, moving forward in time one finds increasingly fewer references to the classic literature in the field and to the various editions of Rogers' volume which has long been considered the standard in the field. At the same time, these new research efforts also have abandoned the constraining survey research methods and are using a wide variety of methods including case studies, ethnographic data, secondary data, and other approaches that are novel, at least in relation to what had been done traditionally.

From the standpoint of basic scientific research, one of the problems with the diffusion of innovations paradigm is that it does not originate in nor fit into any one theoretical tradition. It does not have a theoretical home. In chapter six of this volume Fliegel states that diffusion research never has been theory driven; that it always has been an inductive enterprise. This no doubt reflects its origin and initial rapid growth as an effort to answer questions and provide guidance to the practical problems of modernizing agriculture. The generalizations that resulted from the research were of more immediate importance than the theoretical underpinnings behind them. Reasonable theoretical rationale was provided on a post-hoc basis, and, not surprisingly, there was little theoretical integration. In successive editions of his *Diffusion of Innovations* book Rogers has recognized this lack of a unifying theoretical base and has provided a stronger underlying conceptual framework with a thread that runs through the various elements of the model. The defining concepts of the framework are uncertainty and information. Uncertainty is important to several elements of the model, especially in the adoption-decision process when the potential adopter is unsure about proper use of the innovation and the benefits or costs of its use. Information reduces this uncertainty. The inclusion of the uncertainty-information conceptual scheme certainly has intuitive validity and derives support from several theoretical traditions, but again, it is largely ad hoc theorizing.

NEW DIRECTIONS IN DIFFUSION RESEARCH

Although the diffusion of innovations area of scholarship seems to be languishing, there is a steady, if small, stream of research publications that continues to be issued each year by rural sociologists, sociologists, and other closely related social scientists. Furthermore, regular monitoring of the diffusion of innovations literature over the decade following the most recent of Fliegel's citations has brought to light several new directions or trends in this research tradition. In this section I identify these "innovations" and discuss their methodological and substantive contributions. I will diverge from Fliegel's policy of including only literature within fairly strict confines of rural sociology, by including a few, germane non-rural studies. We can obtain a better understanding of the nature and impact of rural sociology diffusion research by placing it within the context of sociology writ large. Also, Fliegel limited his review to agricultural innovations, whereas I will try to provide a more comprehensive rural overview.

In this endeavor, a question gaining in importance is: What elements constitute any particular piece of published research to be recognized as diffusion of innovations research? At one time this was not a problem in that the key words "adoption," "diffusion," and "innovation" were prominent in the title, and the text of the publication contained a large number of citations to its predecessors from the classic diffusion literature. Neither of these identifiers are necessarily present at this point, especially outside of rural sociology and outside of the United States. What we find is that the primary interest of scholars conducting diffusion research often is not the diffusion process. Their primary interest is in a substantive issue within their own specialty area, and examination of that issue through a diffusion model or process provides explanation of or insight into the issue. Articles reporting on this research may not explicitly identify their diffusion connection, having neither the key words nor familiar citations, but the nature of the issue discussed and the concepts used in the discussion implicitly identify them as belonging to the diffusion of innovations body of literature. Two examples of this genre are Podolny and Stuart's (1995), "A Role-Based Ecology of Technological Change" (sociology), and Clark and Murdock's (1997) "Local Knowledge and the Precarious Extension of Scientific Networks: A Reflection on Three Case Studies" (rural sociology), both to be discussed later.

There are positive and negative aspects to this trend. From the positive side much research is unfettered by existing models and methods of diffusion, and this freedom may result in more creatively conceptualized and executed research. Perhaps ignoring the dominant intellectual paradigm removes the barriers to discovering new and intriguing research questions. Indeed, as we shall see in following discussions, some of the most creative methodological approaches pay little, if any, homage to the classic diffusion of innovations paradigm. On the negative side, if one of the goals of science is to build a cumulative body of knowledge, additivity may be difficult to realize from a number of conceptually unconnected studies. Furthermore, without recognition of what has gone before there may be a good deal of reinvention, not in the diffusion model sense of adopting and changing what exists but in the sense of inventing anew what has gone before.

New directions in diffusion research may be classified into new methods for conducting research and new theoretical and substantive issues addressed by the research. In one sense, these new directions cannot really be called innovative in that they have existed in the research literature. What is new, however, is that they are finally finding their way into rural sociology diffusion research and they are receiving stronger emphasis. Whereas before there may have been a scattered article or two in the literature or some discussion of the need for the using the approach or conducting research on the topic, the methods and issues now are achieving some prominence in the literature.

I will consider two new emphases in methods. First is network analysis used to determine how the structure of relationships in social systems affects innovation diffusion. The second is more generally a movement away from survey research methods to alternative types of data collection strategies that permit understanding the timing and sequence of events of the diffusion process rather than only explaining variation in adoption.

NETWORK ANALYSIS

The effect of the structure of relationships in a social system on the diffusion of innovations has been a major concern of diffusion researchers going back to the beginnings of the development of the model. Early in the model's development the importance of the two-step communication process of information flow into a social system as exemplified by the role of opinion leaders was discovered by diffusion scholars. One of the most significant studies in terms of its contributions to the knowledge in the field and novelty for its time in research methods used was the Coleman et al. (1966) study of the diffusion of a new medical drug among physicians. Coleman and his colleagues extended existing methods of network analysis by actually examining the network linkages and the flow of information about the new drug across those linkages. Over the last decade there have been several more statistically sophisticated reanalyses of Coleman's data with new theoretical interpretations and insights into network relationships and innovation diffusion (Burt, 1987; Strang and Tuma, 1993; Valente, 1995). These reanalyses were made possible, in part, by new computer program packages for network analysis. One of the most comprehensive treatments of network analysis, elaborating on the different types of interpersonal relationships in the structure of a system, the statistical techniques that illuminate those relationships, and the interpretations of the statistics, is Valente's (1995) volume on network models in diffusion. Burt (1999) and Valente and Davis (1999) also provide practical applications resulting from their analyses, although they begin with different theoretical perspectives and end with different conclusions. Valente and Davis (1999) state that opinion leaders are central in a social system or network and their actions influence the actions of others (contagion). They then provide recommendations for recruiting and training opinion leaders for a diffusion program. Burt (1999), on the other hand, proposes that opinion leaders are information brokers and their most important linkages are with other groups. Once the innovation enters the system or network through the opinion leader, diffusion occurs through structural equivalence. Furthermore, by being information brokers, opinion leaders build social capital that results in a competitive advantage within the system.

Search of the rural sociology literature yielded two network analysis studies: one that used formal analytical tools on quantitative data and one that was more informal and qualitative in describing the networks. Warriner and Moul (1992) examined communication network influences on the adoption of agricultural conservation practices. They measured three different structural properties of personal communication networks; connectedness, integration, and diversity. Results indicated that connectedness, or size of the personal communication network and therefore the number of potential sources of new information, was positively related to adoption. Integration, or the extent of reciprocal ties and therefore interlocking and not as open to new information, was negatively related to adoption. Other factors also were important in the adoption of the conservation practices, such as kinship (which will be discussed later), but the research demonstrates that information network structures are important in farmers' adoption of conservation practices.

Coughenour and Chamala (2000) conducted a comparative examination of the process by which conservation tillage systems were developed by farmers in the United States and Australia. They focused on diffusion of tillage systems through local networks involving farmers and institutional change agents. Theirs is a historical analysis involving in-depth event-experience interviews with farmers involved in the development and use of conservation tillage practices, in-depth interviews with organization and agency personnel serving farmers, and published materials such as farm journal articles (Coughenour and Chamala, 2000). They developed and tested an action-learning sequence model in which they posit that the farmer experiences dissonance between the actual outcome of using existing practices and the outcome the farmer ideally would like to achieve. The resolution of the dissonance, the development of a new system of practices, is highly dependent upon the interaction that occurs among farmers and others that constitute the local innovative network (Coughenour and Chamala, 2000).

PROCESS, CASE AND QUALITATIVE STUDIES

As discussed earlier in this chapter, diffusion research in rural sociology, has lived and died by the survey research method. Rogers (1995) makes the distinction between variance research, the traditional quantitative survey research method, and process research, a more qualitative approach needed to understand what occurs and why in the various stages of the diffusion process. Process research is data gathering and analysis that seeks to determine the time-ordered sequence of related events, whereas variance research is data gathering and analysis to determine co-variances and explanatory power of a set of variables (Rogers, 1995). It is only through process research that we come to understand the sequence and nuances of decision-making, and how the transfer of information occurs to spread the innovation through a social system.

Actually, there is considerable published diffusion research in the social sciences using methods other than survey research going back at least two decades. Some researchers have become very innovative in the types of data they have marshaled to test their theories. But in almost all cases the data used are not primary data collected directly from the individuals and groups involved in the diffusion process. Rather they are secondary data such as census type data on population, business, industry, government, and other sectors, collected on a regular basis by government bodies; other data collected by public agencies in the course of their work; published documents of government regulations and legal codes; articles in newspapers, magazines and other publications; and historical documents, both primary and secondary. Some examples will illustrate the innovative use of such data.

Podolny and Stuart (1995) use patents and patent citations to conduct a sophisticated statistical analysis to determine whether an innovation is the basis for future innovation within a technological niche or whether the innovation is a technological dead end. Using the patents and patent citations they examine ties among innovations, those upon which the focal innovation builds and those that have built upon the focal innovation, thus delineating the size of the technological niche. They then examine factors such as the size of the niche, the status of the actors, and the competitive intensity in the niche to determine the focal technology's role as an evolving technology. Lopes (1992) and Walsh (1991) conducted archival research using trade journals as the primary source of data. To examine innovation in the popular music industry Lopes (1992) analyzed the Annual Top 100 hit singles and albums charts from 1969 – 1990 as they appeared in *Billboard*, the most widely read music industry magazine in the United States. Walsh (1991) was interested in the effect of the social context on three innovations in the retail food industry: frozen meat, boxed beef and scanners. For data he used the leading supermarket trade journal, the *Progressive Grocer*, selecting articles dealing with the three innovations from 1950 – 1990, and supplementing this information with interview data from firm managers, union leaders, and workers from two firms in the supermarket industry. In their research on innovation and diffusion of hate crime law in the United States Grattet et al. (1998) used seven published inventories of hate crime legislation. To address diffusion issues such as timing, spatial, and social and cultural proximity, adaptation and re-invention, and continued innovativeness, legal statutes were coded by year of enactment, specific status provisions (eg., race, religion, gender, age) criminal conduct included in each piece of legislation (eg., assault, vandalism, harassment, property damage), and the legal strategies reflected in each statute (eg., criminalizing, interfering with civil rights, penalty enhancement statutes). To test their hypotheses on the diffusion process, they used discrete-time logit event history analysis.

These four examples represent the breadth of research methods and analyses being conducted in the social sciences that are on the cutting edge of diffusion research in terms of examining and explaining the process involved in the adoption and diffusion of innovations. The earlier-mentioned issue of the *Annals* provides further illustrations of these trends. Of ten data-based articles that examine the diffusion of some type of innovation, only two use survey data, and both of these reanalyze the Coleman et al. (1966) data on the diffusion of a medical drug among physicians. The other eight articles are historical analyses using archival data from a variety of different sources, and for the most part they attempt to examine the diffusion process and establish a time-order sequence of events.

Few rural sociologists conducting research on the diffusion of innovations have been able to free themselves from the shackles of survey research methods. Furthermore, there seem to be strong relationships between being a rural sociologists at a United States land grant university where the classic diffusion model was developed, using the model as the departure point for the conceptual basis for research, and the use of survey methods for conducting the research. The examples I found that did not use survey research methods also did not cite the traditional rural sociology diffusion of innovations literature, and the researchers were not based in the U.S. land grant system. These rural sociology studies that do not make reference to the traditional diffusion of innovations literature, like the studies cited above by sociologists, are not so much concerned with developing a model of innovation and diffusion but rather with the meaning and impact of the processes in their own specialty fields of scholarship. Of the five studies concerned with the diffusion process and using alternative research methods I was able to find in the literature I will discuss two here, and the others will be included in later sections of this chapter.

In the first study Clark and Murdoch (1997:39) state that the purpose was to examine the "… relationship between science and other forms of knowledge in local contexts." Science is a social process that remakes the world in its own image, and the findings of science can be duplicated and generalized beyond the area of context of the original studies. The issue of interest for Clark and Murdoch (1997) is what are the implications for existing stocks of local knowledge when science extends itself into new settings. Scientific knowledge can be extended to almost anywhere through its networks, whereas local knowledge is intimately linked to its local context. The study demonstrates that scientific knowledge (innovations within the local context) could more readily meet the scientists' objectives if they recognized the usefulness of existing local knowledge stocks. Using three case studies, Clark and Murdoch (1997) drew upon the published accounts of research by other social scientists; the first being a study of scientific intervention to rejuvenate scallop fishing off the French coast, and the second a study of conflicting local and scientific knowledge on determining the impact of radioactive fallout on sheep in the north of England following the Chernobyl explosion. The third case (Clark and Murdoch, 1997) draws on the authors' own research on the efficacy of scientific recommended practices versus practices based upon years of local farmers' knowledge and experience in conservation. In this case the authors used unstructured in-depth interviews and discussion groups with the farmers, and published documents (more about this case later).

For each of the three cases the authors had sufficient information to document the chronology of events and provide some understanding of why and how different actions occurred when they did. The diffusion of innovations literature, of course, is concerned with the relevance of innovations to specific adopter groups through consideration of the innovation's perceived characteristics and the adopter's need and ability to adopt. Those working in development also have had a long-standing concern with the need and relevance of recommended practices by the target population. What these case studies demonstrate that would not be evident in a cross-sectional survey study is the sequence of the interaction process between the scientists and the local "beneficiaries" of their knowledge. Particularly the increasing loss of credibility of the scientists became evident as scientific knowledge clashed with local knowledge, and the scientific knowledge was found seriously wanting. The scientists exacerbated the problem by maintaining an asymmetrical relationship between scientific and local knowledge, and refusing to accept the potential roles of others to contribute to scientific knowledge.

The second study not following the traditional survey research approach deals with a prominent issue of concern for rural sociologists, the political economy of the development and implementation of new agricultural technologies. Much of this concern initially was spurred by Hightower's (1972) examination of the development of mechanized tomato harvesting. Because of the complexities involved in these macro-processes they do not lend themselves to survey research, at least not without extensive additional data collection using other methods to supplement the survey data. McDonald and Clow (1999) studied the role of technological innovation in mechanization and industrialization of tree harvesting systems in eastern Canada. They interviewed approximately 50 woodworkers, contractors, and woodlands managers of pulp and paper companies. The interviews were of one to four hour duration, and after transcription were analyzed with a computer program called Ethnograph (McDonald and Clow, 1999). They argue against the engineers' explanation of the continued mechanization of the tree cutting as a perpetual process of evolution whereby animate labor was replaced by machines. In the evolution of technology there are successful developments and there are dead ends. Successful machines are those that help restructure and reorganize the division of labor to increase productivity and enable fewer workers to produce the same quantity of wood (McDonald and Clow, 1999). One of the elements in this process was the development of multi-task machines by combining the tasks of single-function machines. Therefore, the driving force of industrialization of the tree harvesting system, revealed through the examination of the sequence of technological innovations and changes in harvesting practices, was not technology development, but rather mechanization of the division of labor to meet the objectives of the employers.

SUBSTANTIVE AREAS IN DIFFUSION RESEARCH

Rogers (1995) states that by the late 1970s rural sociology diffusion publications had dwindled to a few each year, and scholarly attention of diffusion research focused on conservation and other environmental technologies and practices. By then, most of the important theoretical question of the model had been answered. But also, with the increasing surplus food production, the displacement of farm population owing to the increasing scale of farm technology, and the concomitant decline of rural communities, discovering improved methods of technology diffusion hardly seemed justified as a continuing area of research. On the other hand, an area needing research was how to arrest the increasing agricultural problems of soil erosion and water pollution. Was the diffusion of innovations model, which had been developed by research on commercially profitable farming innovations, relevant and useful for explaining the adoption of soil and water conservation practices? Fliegel, who looked upon this topic as an important new direction in diffusion research, stated that the relevance of the diffusion model to environmental innovations had been brought into question in an article by Pampel and van Es (1977). Their argument hinged on the innovation's profitability, that is, the model worked with commercial, profitable innovations but not with environmental, unprofitable innovations.

Pampel and van Es' (1977) publication generated research and discussion on the applicability of the diffusion model by a number of rural sociologists. That debate is reviewed by Fliegel in Chapter 5 of this volume, and therefore it will not be repeated here. Interestingly, though, this area of scholarship has continued to be the primary focus of diffusion research by rural sociologists. A majority of the articles authored by rural sociologists over the last decade that I found in my literature search concerned conservation and other environmental issues. Perhaps this is so because it is a lacuna in diffusion research in which all the intellectual issues have not been resolved. Several new issues have been raised since the initial publication of this book, some of which relate specifically to the environment and conservation, and others that have broader applications.

PROFITABILITY OF INNOVATIONS

Profitability of the innovation has continued to be a prominent objective of inquiry in research on environmental issues. It should be remembered that the important issue with profitability, like other innovation attributes, is its perception by the potential adopter. Saltiel et al. (1994) examined diffusion and farm structure variables to explain variations in farmers' adoption of environmental practices, specifically, sustainable agricultural practices. They found that the perception of long range profitability was the most important variable explaining adoption of the two different types of sustainable systems they examined – management-intensive sustainable practices and low-impact sustainable practices (Saltiel et al., 1994). Perceptions of profitability also were influenced by characteristics of the farm enterprise. Management-intensive systems were considered more profitable by specialized crop producers with large sales, and these producers had an interest, therefore, in building soil tilth. Low-impact systems were considered more profitable by diversified crop-livestock operators, perhaps because of less need or interest in finding an alternative to chemical inputs (Saltiel et al., 1994).

BUNDLED INNOVATIONS

Conducting research on practices such as sustainable agriculture is difficult not only because it is an environmental practice, but also because it is really a bundle or system of practices. Fliegel states that survey research does not lend itself well to bundled technology. Also, in terms of sustainable agriculture, farm operators do not easily fall into mutually exclusive categories of sustainable or conventional. Most operations fall somewhere on a continuum between the two ideal types (Korsching and Malia, 1991). Yet, survey research has been used to examine technology bundles such as sustainable agriculture and integrated pest management (IPM). With technology bundles such as IPM farm operators may ignore recommended practices and they may selectively adopt only those components of the technology with which they are comfortable or that are best suited to their circumstances. Ridgely and Brush (1992) conducted a study of IPM use by pear growers in California. Combining survey data from 64 growers with case studies of four farming operations they found that the important variables explaining extent of adoption of six components of IPM "… reflect the priorities and goals of the farming operation, what is technically feasible for the operation, the source of pest management information, and the value the farmer puts on that information" (Ridgely and Brush, 1992:376). They found that diversified family operations selling to the fresh market are more likely to adopt the beneficial organism components, whereas commercial, less diversified operations are more likely to adopt economic threshold components (Ridgely and Brush, 1992).

Also examining the adoption of IPM, Thomas et al. (1990) take a farming systems approach and define the technology bundle not only by three components of IPM related to growing cotton, but also include the cotton variety grown and the use of irrigation in the technology bundle. Logistics regression on the three components of IPM showed differences in the variables important for explaining the adoption of each component, although belief in the benefits of IPM was significant for all three. Thomas et al. (1990) did not assess why farmers selected or excluded particular practices, but they did take their analysis a step beyond most diffusion research by an examination of the impacts of IPM adoption on per acre yields. Number of IPM practices adopted was a significant variable in regressions predicting per acre yields for both upland and pima cotton (Thomas et al., 1990).

FAMILY, GENDER, AND KINSHIP

Although the influence of the family in the adoption of practices and technologies for the farming operation has been recognized by diffusion researchers, until recently few researchers actually attempted to incorporate the family as a variable into their models. This may be, as Fliegel speculates, because their use of survey research methods made it difficult to incorporate family variables other than from the perspective of the respondent, usually the male family head/farm operator. A notable exception was Abd-Della et al., (1981), an Iowa study of family farms in which both the farm operator and spouse were interviewed.

More recent diffusion of innovations research in rural sociology has become more inclusive of the larger family with special emphasis on the role of women in examination of the adoption process. Ridgely and Brush (1992) mentioned the importance of the family's farming orientation in the adoption of certain components of IPM, a finding derived from follow-up case studies they conducted after collecting survey data. The importance of kinship relationships emerged in the network analysis of the adoption of conservation technologies by Warriner and Moul (1992). The network analysis revealed that structural properties of personal communication networks were influential in conservation technology adoption, and although kin were included in the network structural properties, kin ties had a significant effect independent of network structure. Kin were consulted more often than non-kin on specific farming matters such as cropping and tillage, but having more kin in the personal communication network, although resulting in more consultation, also inhibited innovation (Warriner and Moul, 1992). With more kin in the network there would be fewer opportunities for the introduction of new information.

I turn now to research specifically designed to determine the role of family, gender and kinship in diffusion. Salamon et al. (1997) examined a number of variables including characteristics of husbands and wives and characteristics of the farming operation to determine factors affecting the adoption of sustainable farming systems. They matched 30 sustainable farm operations with 30 conventional farm operations, 10 pairs each in three distinctive soil/weather/predominant enterprise areas of Illinois. Conventional and sustainable farms did not differ significantly in several respects, such as average farm size, soil fertility, crop yields, percent of time allocated to various farming tasks, and wanting to be early adopters of new technologies, but they did differ on other characteristics. Sustainable farmers had more diversified operations, used older tractors with less horsepower, and placed themselves farther on the end of sustainability on a conventional-sustainable scale. Both groups indicated striving toward self-sufficiency, but sustainable farmers defined self-sufficiency with agronomic factors, whereas conventional farmers used economic factors (Salamon et al., 1997). This is where we begin to see the real differences between the two types of farming – in the cultures of the families. The family culture associated with sustainable farming adoption includes " ... family traditions, critical family events with environmental or health consequences, and family resource conservation and frugality patterns" (Salamon et al., 1997:268).

Perhaps nowhere are the issues of intra-household processes of greater consequences for the adoption of innovations than in non-

119

western cultures where the household division of labor, responsibilities for providing sustenance, and property ownership traditionally have definite and clear delineations. In three case studies on intra-household processes in the adoption of hedgerow intercropping in Nigeria and Kenya, David (1998) found that the major factors related to household adoption were the gender division of labor, household decision making, areas of responsibility, and inter-generational land allocation patterns. For example, the decision making on use of the hedgerows may vary depending on areas of responsibility. Hedgerows may have a dual function of improving soil fertility and controlling erosion on the one hand and providing fodder for livestock on the other. Because women are responsible for providing food for the household they may place a high priority on the use of cuttings from hedges for green manure and firewood (David, 1998). Men, on the other hand, are the main owners of livestock and make the decisions on when to sell milk and kill the animals. Therefore, they may place a higher priority on using the hedge cuttings as fodder for livestock (David, 1998). Among the Yoruba where men make the decisions to plant the hedges with the purpose of using cuttings for mulch, women have collection rights on their husbands' land for browse to feed their goats. Thus there is a potential for intra-household conflict over different uses for the foliage (David, 1998). The household head/spouse relationships were much more complicated than these brief examples suggest, and they affected the perceived benefits and costs of the innovations and, in turn, their adoption.

In another example of diffusion research from Kenya Aboud et al. (1996) studied the effect of gender on the adoption of conservation practices by farmer heads of households. They found that although women heads of households were more likely to adopt certain of the conservation practices than men, and there were no significant differences in adoption of the remaining practices, gender was not in itself an important explanatory factor. Gender is a global variable that incorporates other, more directly related factors. " ...gender differences in adoption are being shaped by men's and women's somewhat different conditions and experiences" (Aboud et al., 1996:462). Perhaps there is a proposition here that needs further exploration. Mountjoy (1996) had a similar finding in a study of the relationship between ethnic diversity and the adoption of soil conservation practices by a group of ethnically diverse California strawberry growers. Although ethnic groups varied in their use of soil conservation practices, Mountjoy (1996:353) suggests that "… ethnicity may not be the primary determinant of farming behavior. Instead, the ethnically distinct experiences of strawberry farmers have produced several management styles that now provide a conscious decision-making framework." Both studies imply that gender, ethnic and perhaps other characteristics of potential adopters may not in themselves be the primary drivers of adoption or rejection of an innovation. Rather, it is the accumulation of years, perhaps generations of experiences bracketed by the gender or ethnicity variable that determines the adoption behavior.

INDIGENOUS KNOWLEDGE

Use of the diffusion of innovations model, both in conducting research and in planning and implementing diffusion programs, has been based upon some questionable, if not faulty, assumptions. These have lead to criticisms of diffusion research such as the pro-innovation bias, the individual blame bias, and the problem of equality in the diffusion process and its impacts (Rogers, 1995). There also is a bias for scientific knowledge and against traditional, local, indigenous knowledge. In his criticism of the diffusion of innovations model Busch (1978) suggests the hermeneutic–dialectic (HD) theory as a starting point for revising diffusion of innovations theory.[2] One of the cardinal principles of HD theory is that scientifically derived knowledge is not the only valid knowledge; there are multiple bases for interpreting the world and what is most useful depends on the purposes at hand. "… it (HD) suggests that we take the lifeworlds of other cultures seriously rather than naively assuming the superiority of 'scientific' rationality" (Busch, 1978:469).

Over the last decade rural sociologists have been more attentive to the role of alternative types of knowledge in the diffusion of environmental and other innovations, both here in the U.S. and in other cultures. The already mentioned study by Clark and Murdoch (1997) explicitly demonstrates how the indiscriminate application of scientific knowledge that conflicts with and rejects out of hand the validity of local knowledge can lead to the failure of programs based on that knowledge. By ignoring local knowledge in the implementation of their programs the scientists ignored location specific factors that limited the generalizability of the scientific knowledge, resulting not only in the failure of the program but also in loss of credibility with the local population of scientific knowledge and scientists (Clark and Murdoch, 1997). Thorlindsson (1994) suggests that non-scientists, in their attempts to find improved practices in their work, actually use what amounts to a scientific method of trial and error. Skippers of boats in the Icelandic fishing fleet are constantly experimenting with their boats and equipment and thereby adding innovations to the local stock of knowledge. One of the most notable innovations in herring fishing was the adoption of sonar aboard the fishing boat to locate schools of fish. The first skipper to apply sonar to herring fishing drew upon his own technical skills and knowledge of fishing. "Clearly his approach was not derived from reading textbooks on the scientific method or the logic of scientific inquiry" (Thorlindsson, 1994:338). Now, we have departed somewhat from environmental innovations, but this study does deal with an industry usually considered rural – fishing – and it helps punctuate the point that locally developed knowledge is developed and continues to be used for a reason: it works!

Many of the practices and technologies used in conservation tillage had their origins in on-farm trial-and-error experimentation (Coughenour and Chamala, 2000). Even today, for any of the practices used by operators of sustainable farming systems the primary sources of information are the experiences of other sustainable farmers and the operators' own experiences (Korsching and Malia, 1991). Ashby et al. (1996) found that adoption of soil conservation practices increased significantly when farmers were involved in design of the practices. In a study of the adoption of live soil conservation barriers in Cauca, Colombia, Ashby et al. (1996), used a participatory research design to allow farmers to decide which plants to incorporate into the soil conservation barriers. They found that farmers' criteria for choosing plant varieties differed from the personnel in charge of the program. For example, the short term utility of the plant variety such as having cut-and-carry forage grass and sugar cane for animal fodder was important to the farmers. Comparing farmers who participated in field trips, talked to other farmers, and had the option of selecting their practices, with farmers who had a requirement for using specific practices linked to their use of credit, the voluntary, participatory adopters greatly exceeded the rate of adoption by the obligatory adopters (Ashby et al., 1996).

Ashby et al. (1996:312) conclude "Participatory evaluations of soil conservation techniques can be a powerful tool for improving rates of spontaneous adoption, if farmers' criteria for acceptability are taken into consideration in designing the technology and in formulating recommendations."

INNOVATION IN RESEARCH METHODS

I have devoted considerable discussion to research methods used by rural sociologists for diffusion research. It seems that many continue to use traditional sample survey research designs, but changes are occurring, and researchers are becoming more innovative in their innovation research. Of particular note is the yet unpublished work of Brasier et al. (2000) on farmers use of soil conservation practices. One of the issues with this area of research always has been how to measure the innovativeness of farmers based on the nature of the land needing protection. The typical innovativeness measure consists of a summed scale of the number of practices used by the farmer out of a list of recommended practices.

The validity of such a measure can be seriously challenged when any particular farmer's land may not have features for which some of the practices are appropriate. Brasier et al. (2000) hypothesize that neither the problems of soil erosion nor the behavior of farmers toward soil erosion are evenly distributed. Because of specific locations of problems, specific locations of behaviors, and the interactions between problems and behaviors in specific locations, some groups contribute disproportionately to environmental degradation. The innovativeness of the research is the use of Geographic Information System (GIS) software that allows mapping and analyzing spatial data. When combined with a special statistical package, environmental problems, farmer behavior, and other variables can be linked to and plotted on farm tracts. I will not go into further detail here on what Brasier et al. (2000) are doing in this innovative application of an exciting new tool for researchers. The implications, however, are obvious. From the perspective of researchers and the development of the diffusion of innovations body of knowledge, being able to more precisely link adoption behavior to need for the innovation should help clarify the relationships between adoption and predictor variables.

COMMUNITY INNOVATIVENESS

With few exceptions rural sociologists have not conducted research on the adoption and diffusion of innovations by social systems. Research has focused almost exclusively on adoption and diffusion of innovations by units (individual adopters) within social systems. The diffusion of innovations model, whether in its classic form or as it has been modified more recently, pertains to the micro or individual level, of course. Furthermore, the model, and the primary method used in research with that model, the sample survey, are mutually reinforcing. Thus the model, and the research methods used for its verification, ignore much of the social unit upon which the model was built: the family farm operation. The assumption, largely implicit, always has been that the farm operator/head of household was autonomous in making farm operation decisions. Although data sometimes were collected on other members of the household and/or farming operation, it was the farm operator/head of household that usually provided the information. More recently, as we have seen with the adoption of conservation practices and technologies, the importance of the entire family unit in decision making about the farming operation is being recognized, as is the need for employing research methods other than or in addition to sample surveys.

Rural sociologists and even sociologists until very recently have given little attention to adoption of innovations by social systems and diffusion across systems. Much of that research has been conducted in colleges of business on business organizations and also in education and political science on policy and program diffusion (Rogers, 1995). In sociology, it was largely the organizational ecologists who examined factors leading to organizational innovativeness. Rogers (1995) includes a chapter on organizational innovativeness in his book, but the detail and richness found in the other chapters is lacking.

An area of organizational adoption and diffusion that has received some attention and that is germane owing to the problems experienced by small, rural communities is community adoption of innovations. In an example of such a study Borich and Korsching (1990) examined the importance of several factors leading to community adoption of innovations, with particular focus on the image of the community as held by local residents. Borich and Korsching (1990) combined survey data from two different studies conducted for different purposes, plus secondary data on communities retrieved from several published sources. Two scales were developed to measure the images held by local residents from surveys that used common items in the questionnaires in 22 Iowa communities. The two scales, contentment and fatalism, had previously been shown to be related to innovativeness. Borich and Korsching (1990) transformed individual social psychological variables into group or community attributes through aggregation of individual responses. The measure of innovativeness came from a statewide survey of communities that asked to what degree the communities were sharing with other communities any of a series of 11 services. Sharing of services was considered innovative behavior for small, rural communities with a declining revenue base. The State of Iowa Department of Economic Development was promoting collaboration among rural communities at the time of the study as a method to help them reduce costs and maintain services. These shared services included police and fire protection, landfills and refuse pick up, personnel, purchase and pooling of supplies or equipment, and others. Secondary data were used to measure other typical community characteristics such as per capita income, population change, and per capita local government expenditures. The results indicated that the variables most strongly related to innovativeness were not the size variables usually cited in organizational research, but rather the images of the community as held by its residents (Borich and Korsching, 1990).

Although not a major area of scholarship, other rural sociologists also have studied community innovation. These include Zekeris' (1994) study of the adoption of economic development strategies in rural towns and the Flora and Flora (1990) study of entrepreneurial rural communities. What has not been studied by rural sociologists, however, is diffusion across communities, that is, the process by which the innovation is communicated and spreads throughout a system of communities. Geographers, of course, have long used central place theory and hierarchical diffusion to examine regional and even national diffusion. And more recently, sociologists have used sophisticated statistical techniques such as event history diffusion modeling to examine diffusion across communities. An example is Myers (2000) study of the diffusion of racial rioting in the United States in the years 1964-1971. Gaining an understanding of innovation diffusion across rural communities through the use of these new, powerful statistical techniques could significantly benefit rural development efforts.

INFORMATION SOURCES

Sources of information used by adopters in the adoption decision making process are central to the diffusion model and therefore the subject of a substantial proportion of research reports in this field. Researchers working on the classic diffusion model identified several more-or-less sequential stages in the individual adoption decision-making process. Research further revealed that information sources and channels differed by decision making stage. In the early stages when an individual becomes aware of an innovation secondary, mass media sources, such as newspapers, magazines, or television are most important. As the individual seeks more information, ponders the advisability of adopting the innovation, and finally arrives at a decision, the sources shift to primary, personal sources such as family, friends, and neighbors. The reason for the shift is attributed to the credibility of the source, which has two aspects: The expertise of the source and the source's motivation in providing the information. As the decision on the innovation looms the potential adopter seeks information from sources that are most trustworthy.

Research that established the connection between decision stages and information sources goes back several decades. With the advent of the "information age" has this relationship changed? Organizations that deliver information and education to rural areas, especially the states' Cooperative Extension Services, are attempting to make a shift from personal delivery of information and education to electronic online access to clientele in efforts to reduce expenses in times of shrinking budgets.

How will this play in (the rural areas around) Peoria? Korsching and Hoban (1990) found that among eleven sources of information on conservation, sources that included the relevant public agencies, local sources, and the mass media, the largest percentage of southwestern Iowa farmers (86%) indicated they used farm magazines. Second was peers (other farmers) selected by 82% of the farmers and the third the Soil Conservation Service (SCS) (now the Natural Resources Conservation Service) selected by 77%. Radio and television were fifth (67%) after local papers (72%) and the Agricultural Stabilization and Conservation Service (ASCS) (68%). Farm magazines ranked right behind SCS (ranked first) in being rated most timely or up-to-date and most available, behind SCS and ASCS (ranked first and second) on most knowledgeable, but further back on most trustworthy and most locally relevant. A limitation of their study is that the authors did not inquire about decision-making stage. Saltiel et al. (1994) also found that trade magazines were significant in predicting adoption of sustainable practices in a statewide survey of farmers and ranchers in Montana, although they were more important for low-input practices than management-intensive practices. Professional sources such as extension agents also were important for management-intensive practices (Saltiel et al., 1994). In contradiction to these two studies, the Thomas et al. (1990) study of Texas Cotton growers' adoption of integrated pest management found that sources of information involving interpersonal communication were more important than printed materials in molding IPM beliefs and influencing adoption.

More recently, Lasley et al. (2001) specifically examined preferred educational delivery methods for a statewide sample of Iowa farmers. Because of the availability to farmers of information age technologies and keeping in mind extension's desire to switch to technology-based education delivery methods, farmers were classified low-tech, medium-tech, and high-tech according to their levels of preferred extension use of telecommunications technology (Lasley et al., 2001). Preferred use was measured with a question that asked whether the university should place less, the same amount, or more emphasis on each of 14 information delivery methods. The most preferred methods (with more than or about one-half of respondents in each group indicating they wanted more of these methods) were farmer involvement in applied research, on-farm demonstrations, and news releases via the farm media, with no significant differences across the three groups (Lasley et al., 2001). There were significant differences in computer assisted educational materials and two-way interactive video conferences, with a larger percentage of high-tech farmers wanting more use of these methods. High-tech farmers also wanted significantly more use of local educational meetings, however, and over one-third of all three groups wanted more one-on-one consultations with no significant differences across the three groups (Lasley et al., 2001).

The Thomas et al. (1990) and especially the Lasley et al. (2001) results seem to indicate that despite major inroads by telecommunications into farming, the traditional model of information sources and innovation adoption decision-making still may have relevance. This is one area, however, in which rapid changes are occurring. Abbott et al. (2000) demonstrated that among farmers a critical mass of computers has been achieved and they are now being adopted quickly by the remainder of the farm population. But the uses and impacts of these technologies may be quite different for different size and scale farm operations, as Fliegel suggested. Abbott et al. (2000) found that farmers with larger operations use computers for farm management, whereas smaller farmers tend to used them for family and other non-farm purposes.

Research is needed to determine if the new information technologies that provide almost instant and unlimited information on virtually any topic are changing the adoption and diffusion processes, and, if so, how? The issue, of course, goes far beyond the farm population to encompass the entire rural sector. Information access is no longer space and distance constrained. The hierarchical diffusion model of geographers which posits that innovations originate in the largest urban areas and then diffuse to increasingly smaller communities until the smallest villages are reached may no longer be valid, at least not for communities with state-of-the-art telecommunications technologies. But therein also lies the rub, because to a large extent the diffusion of the infrastructure needed for using innovative telecommunications has followed the geographers' hierarchical model, and many isolated, rural areas are without needed infrastructure and services. Korsching and El-Ghamrini (2000) examined adoption of innovative telephone services by small rural telephone companies. They found that the telephone company's adoption of innovative services for communities in its service area was determined primarily by the company's involvement in local economic development activities. The variable that is usually most important in studies of organizational innovation, size of the organization, added only marginally to the explained variation (Korsching and El-Ghamrini, 2000).

CONSEQUENCES OF INNOVATIONS

Consequences of innovations have received little attention in the research literature. Both Rogers (1995) and Fliegel lament this omission. Not much has changed on this topic over the last decade.

A question that must be addressed at this point is what kinds of impacts or consequences are of interest to sociologist? Some studies asses the impacts of new farm technologies on reduction of soil loss (tons per acre) or gains in productivity (bushels per acre). An example of this is the Thomas et al. (1990) study of the adoption of IPM practices by Texas cotton growers. Thomas et al. (1990) found that IPM adoption resulted in higher per acre yields of both upland and pima cotton. Although the impact of the technology on yields is not a trivial issue, especially for the farmer, the primary interest of sociologists is in the direct or indirect impacts on people – their relationships and their welfare.

In the literature I reviewed only three studies fit this definition of impacts. The first study, already discussed, is Salamon et al. (1997) on factors affecting the adoption of sustainable farming systems. They identify what they call barriers to adoption of sustainable farming systems which are impacts after adoption, such as community pressures from conventional farmers who regard sustainable farmers lazy, poor managers, or busy-work makers, and the anxiety of spouses who are skeptical about sustainable methods and concerned about the future viability of the farming operation (Salamon et al., 1997). The second study by McDonald and Clow (1999) discusses consequences of the technological industrialization of tree harvesting systems on the division of labor and the need for workers. This study falls into a topic that Fliegel identifies as needing more research. "The most important issue, in my opinion, has little to do with mechanization or [firm] size but does involve the extent to which hired labor shares in the benefits of production increases" (p. 59).

The third study by Johnston (1990) is a case study of the introduction of the plow in Timor as an implement for preparing fields for rice cultivation. Plows were introduced to replace the traditional system of tilling the soil for planting which was to drive cattle through the muddy fields in a systematic manner. Problems with the traditional system included, uneven results in turning over soil to a sufficient depth, failure to thoroughly kill the weeds, and the fact that wealthy cattlelords owned and controlled the use of cattle and gained disproportionate financial benefit from this (Johnston, 1990). In the early stages of the program the cattlelords were able to turn the plow program to their benefit, by hiring out cattle with skilled plowmen to the poor farmers who could not afford the cattle to pull the plows. This was finally solved with a credit program for poor farmers. A positive unanticipated consequence that followed is that some of the poor farmers then were able to hire themselves out to plow the fields of other farmers (Johnston, 1990). This case study supports Fliegel's contention that most mechanical innovations are not scale neutral and therefore dependent on the size of the farm enterprise. I would only add that this can apply to even very simple mechanical innovations, depending on the level of sophistication of the social system into which the innovation is introduced.

FAILED INNOVATIONS

Studies of innovations that failed are almost nonexistent (Strang and Soule, 1998). As Rogers (1995) states, failed innovations do not leave a trail to study. The innovation did not diffuse and most traces of it that existed at one time probably have disappeared. Although the innovations are failures diffusion scholars ponder whether there might not be lessons to be learned from studying these innovations to determine what lead to their failure. And indeed, there are lessons to be learned from studying failures, as demonstrated by the two studies found in the literature, one from sociology and one from rural sociology. I won't elaborate on the sociology study other than to say it examined the diffusion of the "shantytown" movement by college and university students in the 1980s as a tactic to persuade their administrations to divest their holdings in South African securities (Soule, 2000). Its most valuable contribution, a theme also found in the rural sociology study (Kremer et al., 2001), was that the entire context of the situation into which an innovation is introduced must be considered to fully understand its success or failure (Soule, 2000).

Kremer et al. (2001) examined the diffusion process of the N-Trak soil nitrogen test kit. The kit, developed by Iowa State University scientists and marketed by a commercial company, allows on-farm testing of the soil for nitrogen available at the early stage of the corn plant growth. The information from the test can be used to derive specific recommendations for nitrogen fertilizer applications, thus potentially reducing production costs and also water pollution. The test generally rates user friendly on all the adoption attributes, or so it seemed, and so successful diffusion was assumed. After encouraging sales the first year, sales quickly declined. Kremer et al. (2001) conducted a comprehensive examination of the N-Trak diffusion process. This included a review of N-Trak literature and existing published research on the kit conducted by rural sociologists, and interviews with ISU scientists, company personnel, extension agents, and farmers who had used the kit.

Kremer et al. (2001) found three major problems with the development process of N-Trak and the research conducted by rural sociologists on its diffusion. First, farmers were not involved in a substantive manner in the research and development process of the innovation. And following from this, the second problem was that the perceived attributes of the innovation were not as favorable as assumed. The main problem was its incompatibility with existing technologies, practices, sequence of operations and time constraints. Finally, the sociological research did not take into consideration the changes in farm structure and social structure that occurred during the diffusion process. Such changes included steadily increasing farm sizes, new options for conducting soil tests, and increasing political pressures to control nitrogen runoff (Kremer et al., 2001).

RE-INVENTION OF INNOVATIONS

Re-invention is defined as the degree to which an innovation is changed or modified by the user in its adoption and implementation (Rogers, 1995). It is not a topic that has caught the fancy of rural sociologists. I usually allot one class period in my diffusion of innovations class to this topic, but rural sociologist's lack of attention to this topic did not really occur to me until recently when I was asked for references to the literature on re-invention of agricultural innovations in the adoption process. To my consternation I had difficulty in providing examples. Almost all the literature on re-invention of innovations comes from education and political science relating to the adoption and diffusion of laws, policies, programs and organizational systems. Studies of concrete technologies (hardware) and specific practices are rare both within and outside of rural sociology.

One can only speculate on reasons for this lack of re-invention research in rural sociology. Certainly re-invention of innovations occurs among farmers and other populations of interest to rural sociologists. Agricultural technologies are modified to fit the needs of the user, and many practices lend themselves to redefinition and modification (Nowak and Korsching, 1985; Coughenour and

Chamala, 2000). Such changes in practices and technologies, whether deliberate or unintentional on the part of the innovator, are sometimes mentioned in the literature but they are not the primary focus of the research. Ridgely and Brush (1992), Ashby et al. (1996), and Thomas et al. (1990) all found some degree of adaptation and selective adoption of conservation technologies and practices by farmers they studied. In each case the innovations were "bundle" technologies, that is, each innovation included several distinctly separate practices and technologies which, when taken together, constitute a system or bundle that yields the highest efficacy or output. Ridgely and Brush (1992) and Thomas et al. (1990) both studied IPM which has several component practices. Farmers varied on the number of components of IPM they adopted. Ashby (1996) studied the adoption of live contour barriers in which farmers could substitute their own desired plants for recommended varieties. These bundle technologies, that by their very nature of having multiple components, each of which has some stand-alone efficacy in addressing the problem, facilitate selective adoption depending on the interests and knowledge of the farmer and the compatibility of the various components with the farming operation (Ridgely and Brush, 1992).

A legitimate question, however, is whether selective adoption of an innovation's components, or adaptation of that innovation to the farming operation is really re-invention. I will not attempt to further define re-invention other than to pose the question, and to pose a further question, why have rural sociologists not concerned themselves more with re-invention? One answer might be that it is a topic which has little theoretical or practical significance. Another possible reason is that the survey research most commonly used does not lend itself to exploring such issues in the adoption process. My inclinations are toward the latter explanation.

CONCLUSION

As I reviewed the diffusion of innovations literature for this chapter two general directions emerged. In one body of literature the researchers sought to maintain a strong tie to the classic diffusion of innovations model while exploring variables or relationships that had either been ignored or had received little attention in the past. Representative of this research are Thomas et al. (1990) who explored the adoption of system or bundled innovations (IPM), and Warriner and Moul (1992) who conducted a network analysis to determine the influence of network structural properties and kinship in the adoption of conservation technologies. Within this genre there also is research that attempts to further refine concepts and relationships of the traditional model to increase their theoretical and methodological utility. As an example, Sapp and Jensen (1997) examined differences in variables predicting symbolic adoption versus use adoption in the intent to eat U.S. beef among Japanese consumers.

In the second body of literature the researchers began with a specific substantive question which involves the diffusion of an innovative technology, practice, or program, framed that question within relevant sociological theory, and drew upon concepts and relationships of the classic diffusion model only as appropriate, if at all. The research by David (1998) did not at all draw upon the classic diffusion model in examining the many complexities of relationships and processes within small farm households in the adoption of hedgerow intercropping. Coughenour and Chamala (2000), on the other hand, did incorporate elements of the classic model and cited relevant extant diffusion literature in their study of farmers' innovations in conservation tillage use. But in development of the theoretical framework for their research, they began not with the diffusion of innovations model, but rather with a model developed from sociological theory that addressed the specific questions guiding their research.

Both avenues of inquiry, extending and refining the classic diffusion of innovations model and exploring new models of innovation diffusion with strong ties to a sociological theoretical base, can provide valuable contributions to our knowledge of the adoption and diffusion processes. Continued research on the classic model, especially with the use of methods not previously considered or sophisticated statistical techniques not formerly available, can help to make it more effective as an analytical and practical tool that provides more detailed insight into how and why diffusion occurs. Regardless of continuing efforts to refine the traditional model, as any other theoretical model it will continue to have shortcomings. Therefore, the findings of research that incorporate alternative theories and models should, when integrated with the findings of research based on the classic model, greatly increase our overall understanding of diffusion processes.

I began this chapter noting that Ruttan (1996) and Rogers (1995) both were pessimistic in their outlook for diffusion of innovations research in rural sociology. I acknowledge that the heyday of diffusion research has ended, but, like Fliegel, I remain optimistic about its future in rural sociology. The introduction of new theories, the application of new methods and statistical techniques, and the exploration of new substantive topics should generate sufficient interest to keep the field viable. Although relatively few rural sociologists may be conducting diffusion of innovations research and their publications may be infrequent, if the past decade's research trends continue, their contributions to the body of knowledge will be substantial. Traditional scholars, however, may need to broaden their concepts of diffusion research.

Notes

1. Citations to Fliegel without further identification refer to earlier chapters of this book.
2. Interestingly, Rogers (1983, 1995) does not mention Busch (1978) in his criticism of the diffusion of innovations model, nor does he mention the hermeneutic-dialectic theory.

References

Abbott, Eric A., J. Paul Yarbrough, and Allan G. Schmidt. 2000. "Farmers, computers, and the Internet: How structures and roles shape the information society." Pp. 201-226 in Peter F. Korsching, Patricia C. Hipple and Eric A. Abbott (eds.) *Having All the Right Connections: Telecommunications and Rural Viability.* Westport, Connecticut: Praeger.

Abd-Ella, Mokhtar M., Eric O. Hoiberg, and Richard D. Warren. 1981. "Adoption behavior in family farm systems: An Iowa study." *Rural Sociology* 46(Spring): 42-61.

Aboud, Abdillahi, Andrew. J. Sofrank, and Serigne Ndiaye. 1996. "The effects of gender on adoption of conservation practices by heads of farm households in Kenya." *Society and Natural Resources* 9:447-463.

Adams, Dale W., and Robert C. Vogel. 1986. "Rural financial markets in low-income countries: Recent controversies and lessons." *World Development* 14 (April):477-487.

Albrecht, Don E., and John K. Thomas. 1986. "Farm tenure: A retest of conventional knowledge." *Rural Sociology* 51 (Spring):18-30.

Ashby, Jacqueline A. 1982. "Technology and ecology: Implications for innovation research in peasant agriculture." *Rural Sociology* 47 (Summer):234-250.

---------. 1985. "The social ecology of soil erosion in a Colombian farming system." *Rural Sociology* 50 (Fall):377-396.

References

Ashby, Jacqueline A., Jorge Alonso Beltrán, Maira del Pilar Guerrero, and Hector Fabio Ramos. 1996. "Improving the acceptability to farmers of soil conservation practices." *Journal of Soil and Water Conservation* 51(4):309-312.

Audirac, Ivonne, and Lionel J. Beaulieu. 1986. "Microcomputers in agriculture: A proposed model to study their diffusion/adoption." *Rural Sociology* 51 (Spring):60-77.

Barnes, Douglas, and Reeve Vanneman. 1983. "Agricultural development and rural landlessness in India." *Studies in Comparative International Development* 18 (Spring-Summer):90-112.

Barnett, H. G. 1953. *Innovation: The Basis of Cultural Change.* New York:McGraw-Hill.

Beal, George M., and Joe E. Bohlen. 1957. *The Diffusion Process.* Ames, Iowa: Iowa State College, Agricultural Extension Service, Special Report 18.

Bealer, Robert C., and Joyce M. Kling. 1975. "Cumulative index, volumes 31-40: 1966-1975." *Rural Sociology* 40 (Winter): supplement to Winter 1975 issue.

Berardi, Gigi M. 1981. "Socio-economic consequences of agricultural mechanization in the United States: Needed redirections for mechanization research." *Rural Sociology* 46:483-504.

Berardi, Gigi M., and Charles C. Geisler (eds.). 1984. *The Social Consequences and Challenges of New Agricultural Technologies.* Boulder, Colorado: Westview Press.

Binswanger, Hans P. 1984. *Agricultural Mechanization: A Comparative Historical Perspective.* Washington, D.C.: The World Bank, World Bank Staff Working Papers No. 673.

Borich, Timothy O. and Peter F. Korsching. 1990. "Community image and community innovativeness." *Journal of the Community Development Society* 21(1):1-18.

Bose, S. P. 1964. *The Adopters.* Calcutta, India: Government of West Bengal, Department of Agriculture and Community Development, Extension Bulletin No. 2.

Brasier, Kathryn, Pete Nowak, Perry Cabot, and Bruce Kahn. 2000. "Bringing space into agriculture-environment relations." Unpublished working paper. Department of Sociology, University of Wisconsin, Madison, Wisconsin.

Brown, Lawrence A. 1981. *Innovation Diffusion: A New Perspective.* New York: Methuen.

References

Brown, Lawrence A., Edward J. Malecki, and Aron N. Spector. 1976. "Adopter categories in a spatial context: Alternative explanations for an empirical regularity." *Rural Sociology* 41 (Spring):99-118.

Burt, Ronald S. 1987. "Social contagion and innovation, cohesion versus structural equivalence." *American Journal of Sociology* 92:1287-1335.

--------. 1999. "The social capital of opinion leaders." *The Annals of the American Academy of Political and Social Science* 569(May):37-54.

Busch, Lawrence. 1978. "On understanding understanding: Two views of communication." *Rural Sociology* 43(3): 450-473.

Buttel, Frederick H. 1983. "Beyond the family farm." Pp. 87-107 in Gene F. Summers (ed.) *Technology and Social Change in Rural Areas.* Boulder, Colorado: Westview Press.

Buttel, Frederick H., Gilbert W. Gillespie, Jr., Oscar W. Larson, III, and Craig K. Harris. 1981. "The social bases of agrarian environmentalism: A comparative analysis of New York and Michigan farm operators." *Rural Sociology* 46 (Fall):391-410.

Buttel, Frederick H., Gilbert W. Gillespie, Jr., Rhonda Janke, Brian Caldwell, and Marriane Sarrantonio. 1986. "Reduced-input agricultural systems: A critique." *The Rural Sociologists* 6 (September):350-370.

Buttel, Frederick H., Martin Kenney, and Jack Kloppenburg, Jr. 1985. "From green revolution to biorevolution: Some observations on the changing technological bases of economic transformation in the third world." *Economic Development and Cultural Change* 34 (October):31-55.

Buttel, Frederick H., and Oscar W. Larson, III. 1979. "Farm size, structure, and energy intensity: An ecological analysis of U.S. agriculture." *Rural Sociology* 44 (Fall):471-488.

Cancian, Frank. 1967. "Stratification and risk-taking: A theory tested on agricultural innovation." *American Sociological Review* 32 (December):912-927.

--------. 1979. *The Innovator's Situation: Upper-Middle-Class Conservatism in Agricultural Communities.* Stanford, California: Stanford University Press.

--------. 1981. "Community of reference in rural stratification research." *Rural Sociology* 46 (Winter):626-645.

References

Carlson, John E., and Don A. Dillman. 1983. "Influence of kinship arrangement on farmers' innovativeness." *Rural Sociology* 48 (Summer):183-200.

--------. 1988. "The influence of farmers' mechanical skill on the development and adoption of a new agricultural practice." *Rural Sociology* 53 (2):235-245.

Carlson, John E., Don A. Dillman, and C. Ellen Lamiman. 1987. *The Present and Future Use of No-Till in the Palouse.* Research Bulletin No. 140. Moscow, Idaho: University of Idaho, Agricultural Experiment Station.

Carlson, John E., Barbara Schnabel, Curtis E. Beus, and Don A. Dillman. 1992. "Changes in soil conservation attitudes and behaviors in the Palouse and Camas Prairies: 1976-1990." Unpublished.

Chapin F. Stuart. 1928. Cultural Change. New York: Century Company.

Christenson, James A., and Lorraine E. Garkovich. 1985. "Fifty years of *Rural Sociology:* Status, trends, and impressions." *Rural Sociology* 50 (Winter):503-522.

Clark, Judy and Jonathan Murdoch. 1997. "Local knowledge and the precarious extension of scientific networks: A reflection on three case studies. *Sociologia Ruralis* 37(1):38-60.

Cochrane, Willard W. 1958. *Farm Prices: Myth and Reality.* Minneapolis, Minnesota: University of Minnesota Press.

Coleman, James S., Elihu Katz, and Herbert Menzel. 1966. *Medical Innovation.* New York: Bobbs-Merrill.

Comis, Don. 1986. "Where Comax speaks, farmers listen." *Agricultural Research* 34 (September):6-10.

Copp, James H. 1984. "Agricultural mechanization: Physical and societal effects and implications for policy development." Pp. 237-248 in Gigi M. Berardi and Charles C. Geisler (eds.). *The Social Consequences and Challenges of New Agricultural Technologies.* Boulder, Colorado: Westview Press.

Copp, James H., Maurice L. Still, and Emory J. Brown. 1958. "The function of information sources in the farm practice adoption process." *Rural Sociology* 23 (June):146-157.

Coughenour, C. Milton. 1965. "The problem of reliability of adoption data in survey research." *Rural Sociology* 30 (June):184-203.

References

Coughenour, C. Milton and Shankariah Chamala. 2000. *Conservation Tillage and Cropping Innovation: Constructing the New Culture of Agriculture.* Ames, Iowa: Iowa State University Press

Council for Agricultural Science and Technology. 1983. *Agricultural Mechanization: Physical and Societal Effects, and Implications for Policy Development.* CAST Report No. 96. Ames, Iowa: Council for Agricultural Science and Technology.

David, Soniia. 1998. "Intra-household processes and the adoption of hedgerow intercropping." *Agriculture and Human Values* 15:31-42.

deJanvry, Alain, and Jean-Jacques Dethier. 1985. *Technological Innovation in Agriculture: The Political Economy of its Rate and Bias.* OGIAR Study Paper Number 1. Washington, D.C.: The World Bank.

Dillman, Don A., and John E. Carlson. 1982. "Influence of absentee landlords on soil erosion and control practices." *Journal of Soil and Water Conservation* 37 (January-February):37-41.

Domer, Peter. 1983. "Technology and U.S. agriculture." Pp. 73-88 in Gene F. Summers (ed.), *Technology and Social Change in Rural Areas.* Boulder, Colorado: Westview Press.

Doorman, Frans. 1991. "A framework for the rapid appraisal of factors that influence the adoption and impact of new agricultural technology." *Human Organization* 50(3):235-244.

Duncan, James A., and Burton W. Kreitlow. 1954. "Selected cultural characteristics and the acceptance of education programs and practices." *Rural Sociology* (December):349-357.

Feder, Gershon, Richard E. Just, and David Zilberman. 1985. "Adoption of agricultural innovations in developing countries: A survey." *Economic Development and Cultural Change* 33 (January):255-298.

Firey, Walter. 1984. "The small farm and the conservation of natural resources: A problem in theory construction and application." *The Rural Sociologist* 4 (November):396-403.

Fliegel, Frederick C. 1956. "A multiple correlation analysis of factors associated with adoption of farm practices." *Rural Sociology* 21 (September-December):284-292.

References

--------. 1966. "Literacy and exposure to instrumental information among farmers in southern Brazil." *Rural Sociology* 31 (March):15-28.

Fliegel, Frederick C., and Joseph E. Kivlin. 1962a. *Differences Among Improved Farm Practices as Related to Rates of Adoption.* University Park, Pennsylvania: Pennsylvania State University Agricultural Experiment Station Bulletin 691.

--------. 1962b. "Farm practice attributes and adoption rates." *Social Forces* 40 (June):364-370.

--------. 1966. "Farmers' perceptions of farm practice attributes." *Rural Sociology* 31 (June):197-206.

Fliegel, Frederick C., Joseph E. Kivlin, and Gurmeet S. Sekhon. 1968. "A cross-national comparison of farmers' perception of innovations as related to adoption behavior." *Rural Sociology* 33 (December):437-449.

Fliegel, Frederick C., and Manoel M. Tourinho. 1985. "Ambient social consequences of technological modernization: Southern Bahia." Paper presented at the annual meeting of the American Association for the Advancement of Science, Los Angeles, California.

Fliegel, Frederick C., and J. C. van Es. 1983. "The diffusion-adoption process in agriculture: Changes in technology and change in paradigms." Pp. 13-28 in Gene F. Summers (ed.), *Technology and Social Change in Rural Areas.* Boulder, Colorado: Westview Press.

Flora, Cornelia Butler and Jan L. Flora. 1990. "Developing entrepreneurial rural communities." *Sociological Practice* 8:197-207.

Frankel, Francine. 1971. *India's Green Revolution: Economic Gains and Political Costs.* Princeton, New Jersey: Princeton University Press.

Fredericks, Anne. 1984. "Technological change and the growth of agribusiness: A case study of California lettuce production." Pp. 249-264 in Gigi M. Berardi and Charles C. Geisler (eds.), *The Social Consequences and Challenges of New Agricultural Technologies.* Boulder, Colorado: Westview Press.

Freeman, David M., Hosein Azadi, and Max K. Lowdermilk. 1982. "Power distribution and adoption of agricultural innovations:

References

A structural analysis of villages in Pakistan." *Rural Sociology* 47 (Spring):68-80.

Friedland, William H. 1984. "A programmatic approach to the social impact assessment of agricultural technology." Pp. 197-212 in Gigi M. Berardi and Charles C. Geisler (eds.), *The Social Consequences and Challenges of New Agricultural Technologies.* Boulder, Colorado: Westview Press.

Friedland, William H., Amy Barton, and R. J. Thomas. 1981. *Manufacturing Green Gold: Capital, Labor, and Technology in the Lettuce Industry.* New York: Cambridge.

Galjart, Benno. 1971. "Rural development and sociological concepts: A critique." *Rural Sociology* 36 (March):31-41.

Garg, Om Prakash, and H. L. Srivastava. 1972. "Impact of modern technology and rural unemployment." *Indian Journal of Agricultural Economics* 27 (October-December):206-210.

Garkovich, Lorraine. 1985. "50-year index, volumes 1-50, 1936-1985." *Rural Sociology* 50 (Winter): supplement to Winter 1985 issue.

Gartrell, C. David, and John W. Gartrell. 1985. "Social status and agricultural innovation: A meta-analysis." *Rural Sociology* 50 (Spring):38-50.

Goss, Kevin F. 1979. "Consequences of diffusion of innovations." *Rural Sociology* 44 (Winter):754-772.

Gotsch, Carl H. 1972. "Technical change and the distribution of income in rural areas." *American Journal of Agricultural Economics* 54 (May):326-341.

Grattet, Ryken, Valerie Jennes, and Theodore R. Curry. 1998. "The homogenization and differentiation of hate crime law in the United States, 1978 to 1995: Innovation and diffusion in the criminalization of bigotry." *American Sociological Review* 63(April):286-307.

Gross, Neal. 1949. "The differential characteristics of acceptors and non-acceptors of an approved agricultural technological practice." *Rural Sociology* 14 (June):148-158.

Gross, Neal, and Marvin J. Taves. 1952. "Characteristics associated with acceptance of recommended farm practices." *Rural Sociology* 17 (December):321-327.

Gusfield, Joseph R. 1967. "Tradition and modernity: Misplaced polarities in the study of social change." *American Journal of Sociology* 72 (January):351-362.

References

Havens, A. Eugene. 1975. "Diffusion of new seed varieties and its consequences: A Colombian case." Pp. 93-111 in Raymond E. Dumett and Lawrence J. Brainard (eds.), *Problems of Rural Development*. Leiden, The Netherlands: E. J. Brill.

Havens, A. Eugene, and William L. Flinn. 1975. "Green revolution technology and community development: The limits of action programs." *Economic Development and Cultural Change* 23 (April):469-481.

Hayami, Yujiro, and Vernon W. Ruttan. 1971. *Agricultural Development: An International Perspective*. Baltimore: The Johns Hopkins University Press.

Heaton, Tim B., and David L. Brown. 1982. "Farm structure and energy intensity: Another look." *Rural Sociology* 47 (Spring):17-31.

Heffernan, William D., and Gary P. Green. 1986. "Farm size and soil loss: Prospects for a sustainable agriculture." *Rural Sociology* 51 (Spring):31-42.

Hightower, James. 1972. *Hard Tomatoes, Hard Times: The Failure of America's Land Grant College Complex*. Cambridge, Massachusetts: Schenkman.

Hoffer, Charles R. 1942. *Acceptance of Approved Farming Practices Among Farmers of Dutch Descent*. East Lansing, Michigan: Michigan State College Agricultural Experiment Station, Special Bulletin 316.

Johnson, Eldon L. 1985. "Some development lessons from the early land-grant colleges." *The Journal of the Developing Areas* 19 (January):139-148.

Johnson, S.S., and M. Zahara. 1976. "Prospective lettuce harvest mechanization: Impact on labor." *Journal of American Sociological Horticulture Science* 101 (4):378-381.

Johnston, Mary. 1990. "Dilemmas in introducing applied technology: The plough and the cattlelords in Timor." *Community Development Journal* 25(3):243-251.

Korsching, Peter F. and Sami El-Ghamrini. 2000. "Telephone companies: Providing all the right connections for viable rural communities." Pp. 39-60 in Peter F. Korsching, Patricia C. Hipple and Eric. A. Abbott (eds.) *Having All the Right Connections: Telecommunications and Rural Viability*. Westport, Connecticut: Praeger.

References

Korsching, Peter F. and Thomas J. Hoban, IV. 1990. "Relationship between information sources and farmers' conservation perceptions and behavior." *Society and Natural Resources* 3:1-10.

Korsching, Peter F. and James E. Malia. 1991. "Institutional support for practicing sustainable agriculture." *American Journal of Alternative Agriculture* 6(1):17-22.

Kremer, Kathy S., Michael Carolan, Stephen Gasteyer, S. Noor Tirmizi, Peter F. Korsching, Gregory Peter, and Pingsheng Tong. 2000. "Evolution of an agricultural innovation: The N-Trak soil nitrogen test – adopt and discontinue, or reject?" *Technology in Society* (Forthcoming).

Lantz, Herman R. 1984. "Continuities and discontinuities in American sociology." *The Sociological Quarterly* 25 (Autumn):581-596.

Lasley, Paul, and Gordon Bultena. 1986. "Farmers' opinions about third-wave technologies." *American Journal of Alternative Agriculture* 1 (Summer):122-126.

Lasley, Paul, Steve Padgitt, and Margie Hanson. 2000. "Implications of the telecommunications age on farmers and extension." *Technology in Society* (Forthcoming).

Lemmon, Hal. 1986. "Comax: An expert system for cotton crop management." *Science* 233 (4 July):29-33.

Lenski, Gerhard, and Patrick D. Nolan. 1984. "Trajectories of development: A test of ecological-evolutionary theory." *Social Forces* 63 (September):1-23.

Lerner, Daniel. 1958. *The Passing of Traditional Society: Modernizing the Middle East.* New York: Free Press.

Lionberger, Herbert F. 1960. *Adoption of New Ideas and Practices.* Ames, Iowa: Iowa State University Press.

Lipton, Michael, and Richard Longhurst. 1985. *Modern Varieties, International Agricultural Research, and the Poor.* OGIAR Study Paper No. 2. Washington, D.C.: The World Bank.

Loomis, Charles P., and John C. McKinney. 1956. "Systemic differences between Latin-American communities of family farms and large estates." *American Journal of Sociology* 61 (March):404-412.

Lopes, Paul D. 1992. "Innovation and diversity in the popular music industry, 1969 to 1990." *American Sociological Review* 57(February):56-71.

References

MacDonald, Peter and Michael Clow. 1999. "'Just one damn machine after another?' Technological innovation and the industrialization of tree harvesting systems." *Technology in Society* 21:323-344.

Marsh, C. Paul, and A. Lee Coleman. 1954. "The relation of neighborhood of residence to adoption of recommended practices." *Rural Sociology* 19 (December):385-389.

Morrison, Denton E. 1983. "Soft tech/hard tech, hi tech/lo tech: A social movement analysis of appropriate technology." *Sociological Inquiry* 53 (Spring-Summer):220-251.

Mountjoy, Daniel C. 1996. "Ethnic diversity and the patterned adoption of soil conservation in the Strawberry Hills of Monterey, California." *Society and Natural Resources* 9:339-357.

Myers, Daniel J. 2000. "The diffusion of collective violence: Infectiousness, susceptibility, and mass media networks." *American Journal of Sociology* 106(1):173-208.

Nolan, Patrick D., and Gerhard Lenski. 1985. "Technoeconomic heritage, patterns of development, and the advantages of backwardness." *Social Forces* 64 (December):341-358.

North Central Rural Sociology Committee. 1955. *How Farm People Accept New Ideas.* Ames, Iowa: Iowa State College Agricultural Extension Service, North Central Regional Publication No. 1 of the Agricultural Extension Services.

--------. 1956. *Bibliography of Research on: Social Factors in the Adoption of Farm Practices.* Ames, Iowa: Iowa State College, supplement to North Central Regional Publication No. 1.

--------. 1961. *Adopters of New Farm Ideas: Characteristics and Communication Behavior.* East Lansing, Michigan: Michigan State University, Cooperative Extension Service, North Central Regional Extension Publication No. 13.

Nowak, Peter J. 1983. "Adoption and diffusion of soil and water conservation practices." *The Rural Sociologist* 3 (March):83-91.

--------. 1987. "The adoption of agricultural conservation technologies: Economic and diffusion explanations." *Rural Sociology* 52 (2):208-220.

References

Nowak, Peter J., and Peter F. Korsching. 1985. "Conservation tillage: Revolutionary or evolutionary." *Journal of Soil and Water Conservation* 40 (March-April):199-201.

O'Hearn, Denis. 1994. "Innovation and the world-system hierarchy: British subjugation of the Irish cotton industry, 1780-1830." *American Journal of Sociology* 100(3):587-621.

Ogburn, William F. 1922. *Social Change with Respect to Culture and Original Nature.* New York: B.W. Huebsch.

--------. 1957. "Cultural lag as theory." *Sociology and Social Research* 41 (January-February):167-174.

Pampel, Fred, Jr., and J. C. van Es. 1977. "Environmental quality and issues of adoption research." *Rural Sociology* 42 (Spring):57-71.

Pedersen, Harold A. 1951. "Cultural differences in the acceptance of recommended practices." *Rural Sociology* 16 (March):37-49.

Podolny, Joel M. and Toby E. Stuart. 1995. "A role-based ecology of technological change. *American Journal of Sociology* 5(March):1224-1260.

Rhoades, Robert E. 1984. *Breaking New Ground—Anthropology in Agricultural Research.* Lima, Peru: International Potato Center (CIP).

Ridgely, Anne-Marie and Stephen B. Brush. 1992. "Social factors and selective technology adoption: The case of integrated pest management." *Human Organization* 51(4):367-378.

Rogers, Everett M. 1958. "Categorizing the adopters of agricultural practices." *Rural Sociology* 23 (December):345-354.

--------. 1962. *Diffusion of Innovations.* New York: Free Press of Glencoe.

--------. 1976. "Communication and development: The passing of a dominant paradigm." *Communications Research* 3 (April):213-240.

--------. 1983. *Diffusion of Innovations.* Third Edition. New York: Free Press.

--------. 1995. *Diffusion of Innovations.* Fourth Edition. New York: Free Press.

Rogers, Everett M., and L. Edna Rogers. 1961. "A methodological analysis of adoption scales." *Rural Sociology* 26 (December):325-336.

References

Rogers, Everett M., and Wicky L. Meynen. 1965. "Communication sources for 2,4-D weed spray among Colombian peasants." *Rural Sociology* 30 (June):213-219.

Rogers, Everett M., with F. Floyd Shoemaker. 1971. *Communication of Innovations: A Cross-Cultural Approach.* New York: Free Press.

Rossi, Peter H., Howard E. Freeman, and Sonia R. Wright. 1979. *Evaluation: A Systematic Approach.* Beverly Hills, California: Sage Publications, Inc.

Ruttan, Vernon W. 1977. "The green revolution: Seven generalizations." *International Development Review* 19 (December):16-23.

--------. 1982. "Changing role of public and private sectors in agricultural research." *Science* 216 (2 April):23-29.

--------. 1983. "The global agricultural support system." *Science* 222 (7 October):11.

--------. 1996. "What happened to technology adoption-diffusion research?" *Sociologia Ruralis* 36(1):51-73.

Ryan, Bryce. 1948. "A study in technological diffusion." *Rural Sociology* 13 (September):273-285.

Ryan, Bryce, and Neal Gross. 1943. "The diffusion of hybrid seed corn." *Rural Sociology* 8 (March):15-24.

Saint, William S., and E. Walter Coward. 1977. "Agriculture and behavioral science: Emerging orientations." *Science* 197 (19 August):733-737.

Salamon, Sonya, Richard L. Farnsworth, Donald G. Bullock and Raji Yusuf. 1997. "Family factors affecting adoption of sustainable farming systems." *Journal of Soil and Water Conservation* 52(2):265-271.

Saltiel, John, James W. Bauder, and Sandy Palakovich. 1994. "Adoption of sustainable agricultural practices: Diffusion, farm structure, and profitability." *Rural Sociology* 59(Summer):333-349.

Sapp, Stephen G. and Helen H. Jensen. 1997. "Socioeconomic impacts on implementation and confirmation decisions: Adoption of U.S. beef in Japan." *Rural Sociology* 62(Winter):508-524.

References

Schmitz, Andrew, and David Seckler. 1984. "Agriculture and social welfare: The case of the tomato harvester." Pp. 103-119 in Gigi M. Berardi and Charles C. Geisler (eds.), *The Social Consequences and Challenges of New Agriculture Technologies.* Boulder, Colorado: Westview Press.

Schneider, Keith. 1986. "Biotech's stalled revolution." *The New York Times Magazine* (16 November):42-44 et passim.

Schultz, Theodore W. 1964. *Transforming Traditional Agriculture.* New Haven, Connecticut: Yale University Press.

Shingi, Prakash M., Frederick C. Fliegel, and Joseph E. Kivlin. 1981. "Agricultural technology and the issue of unequal distribution of rewards: An Indian case study." *Rural Sociology* 46 (Fall):430-445.

Shingi, Prakash M., Gurinder Kaur, and Ravi Prakash Rai. 1982. *Television and Knowledge-Gap Hypotheses.* Ahmedabad, India: Centre for Management in Agriculture, Indian Institute of Management.

Sidhu, Surjit S. 1974. "Relative efficiency of wheat production in the Indian Punjab." *The American Economic Review* 64 (September):742-751.

Soule, Sarah A. 1999. "The diffusion of an unsuccessful innovation." *The Annals of the American Academy of Political and Social Science* 569(May):120-131.

Stockdale, J.D. 1977. "Technology and change in United States agriculture: Model or warning?" *Sociologia Ruralis* 17 (Nos. 1 and 2):43-58.

Stokes, C. Shannon, and Michael K. Miller. 1985. "A methodological review of fifty years of research in *Rural Sociology.*" *Rural Sociology* 50 (Winter):539-560.

Strang, David and Sarah A. Soule. 1998. "Diffusion in organizations and social movements: From hybrid corn to poison pills." *Annual Review of Sociology* 24:265-290.

Strang, David and Nancy B. Tuma. 1993. "Spatial and temporal heterogeneity in diffusion." *American Journal of Sociology* 99:614-639.

Summers, Gene F. 1983. "The future of rural sociology: An introduction." *The Rural Sociologist* 3 (September):312-314.

Sun, Marjorie. 1986. "Will growth hormone swell milk surplus?" *Science* 233 (11 July):150-151.

References

Swenson, C. Geoffrey. 1976. "The distribution of benefits from increased rice production in Thanjavur District, South India." *Indian Journal of Agricultural Economics* 31 (January-March):1-12.

Thomas, John K., Howard Ladewig and Wm. Alex McIntosh. 1990. "The adoption of integrated pest management practices among Texas cotton growers." *Rural Sociology* 55(Fall):395-410.

Thorlindsson, Thoralfur. 1994. "Skipper science: A note on the epistemology of practice and the nature of expertise." *Sociological Quarterly* 35(2):329-345.

Tichenor, P.J., G. A. Donohue, and C. N. Olien. 1970. "Mass media flow and differential growth in knowledge." *Public Opinion Quarterly* 34 (Summer):159-170.

Tweeten, Luther. 1986. "Agricultural technology—the potential socioeconomic impact." Paper presented to the Oklahoma Network for Continuing Higher Education Leadership Development Seminar. Stillwater, Oklahoma: Oklahoma State University.

Valente, Thomas. 1995. *Network Models of Diffusion of Innovativeness.* Cresskill, New Jersey:Hampton Press.

Valente, Thomas W. and Rebecca L. Davis. 1999. "Accelerating the diffusion of innovations using opinion leaders." *The Annals of the American Academy of Political and Social Science* 569(May):55-67.

van Es, J. C. 1983. "The adoption/diffusion tradition applied to resource conservation: Inappropriate use of existing knowledge." *The Rural Sociologist* 3 (March):76-82.

van Es. J. C., and Theodore Tsoukalas. 1987. "Kinship arrangements and innovativeness: A comparison of Palouse and Prairie findings." *Rural Sociology* 52 (3):389-397.

Walsh, John P. 1991. "The social context of technological change: The case of the retail food industry." *Sociological Quarterly* 32(3):447-468.

Ward, Gerald M., Thomas M. Sutherland, and Jean M. Sutherland. 1980. "Animals as an energy source in third world agriculture." *Science* 208 (9 May):570-574.

Warland, Rex. 1988. "Rural Sociology Society 1988 Annual Awards Banquet." *The Rural Sociologist* 8 (5):439-445.

References

Warriner, G. Keith and Trudy M. Moul. 1992. "Kinship and personal communication network influences on the adoption of agricultural conservation technology." *Journal of Rural Studies* 8(3):279-291.

Whyte, William Foote. 1985. Review of Gene F. Summers (ed.), *Technology and Social Change in Rural Areas. Contemporary Sociology* 14 (January):65.

Wilkening, Eugene A. 1950. "Sources of information for improved farm practices." *Rural Sociology* 15 (March):19-30.

--------. 1953. *Adoption of Improved Farm Practices.* Madison, Wisconsin: University of Wisconsin Agricultural Experiment Station, Research Bulletin 183.

Wilkening, Eugene A., and Lakshmi K. Bharadwaj. 1968. "Aspirations and task involvement as related to decision-making among farm husbands and wives." *Rural Sociology* 33 (March):30-45.

Wilkening, Eugene A., and Sylvia Guerrero. 1969. "Consensus in aspirations for farm improvements and adoption of farm practices." *Rural Sociology* 34 (June):182-196.

Wilkening, Eugene A., Joan Tully, and Hartley Presser. 1962. "Communication and acceptance of recommended farm practices among dairy farmers in Northern Victoria." *Rural Sociology* 27 (June):116-197.

Zekeri, Andrew. 1994. "Adoption of economic development strategies in small towns and rural areas: Effects of past community action." *Journal of Rural Studies* 10(2):185-195.

References

INDEX

farm operation characteristics and, 119; gender and, 120; household division of labor and, 119; kinship relations and, 111; outside of agriculture, 36; role of women and, 118; social structure and, 44-45, 87, 94; tenure status and, 7, 15, 45, 57, 74, 89

Adoption process: information sources and, 28, 40-42, 125-128; stages, 25-28, 125, 126

Adoption rates, locality groups and, 35-36

Adoption scales, 18

Analytical techniques, 125; discrete-time logit event history analysis, 113; Ethnograph, 115; Geographic Information System, 123; logistic regression, 118; network analysis, 109-111

Annals of the American Academy of Political and Social Science, 106, 113

Appropriate technology, 19, 38, 66, 78-79

Attributes of innovations, 28-34, 67, 84

Biotechnology, 97-98, 101, 102

Bovine growth hormone, 101-102

Cancian, Frank, 80-83

Capital intensity, 34, 56, 63; scale neutrality and, 56-58;

use of resources and, 66, 72-77

Central place theory, 125

Chapin, F. Stuart, 4-5, 11

Classical model of diffusion research, 14-16, critique, 52-54, 62, 121; modifications of, 68; social structure and, 44-45

Comax, 98, 99, 100-102

Communications approach to diffusion research, 6, 25-28, 40-46, 69, 93; in the third world, 40-46

Communication two-step process, 110

Community innovativeness, 123-125

Computer use, farmer, 127

Consequences of adoption, 48, 56-64, 100

Consequences of technological change, 56-64; call for specification of, 61-62; regional differences and, 61; scale neutrality and, 57-58

Conservation technology, 66-79, 122, 131; the landlord-tenant relationship and, 74-77

Conservation tillage, 111

Credit availability, 53-54, 58, 129

Cultural lag hypothesis, 1, 3-4, 11

Data: archival, 112, 113; census, 112; secondary, 112

Diffusion curve, 4-5, 7, 10-11, 21, 22

Information transfer: face-to-face, 41, 43; in the third world, 40-46; literacy and, 42-44

Information technologies, 127

Information: role in reducing uncertainty, 107

Information flows, 15-16, 20, 41

Information sources, 41-42, 125-128; credibility of, 126; primary and secondary, 126, 127

Innovations: attributes of, 28-34, 67, 84, 130; bundled, 117, 118, 131; classification of, 8, 34; failed, 129, 130; packages, 48, 84-85, 87, 100; profitability, 116, 117

Innovativeness: in the fishing industry 121-122; as a personality trait, 16-19, 20, 22-23, 78, 84; measures of, 18, 42, 67, 78, 83-84, 99

Innovators, 22, 42

Integrated pest management, 117, 118, 126, 128, 131

Iowa State hybrid corn studies, 1, 3, 6-9, 16

Knowledge: indigenous, 121, 122; local, 114, 121; local versus scientific, 114, 121; scientific 114, 121

Laggards, 43, 52

Land grant system, 11, 113

Lerner, Daniel, 43

Lionberger, Herbert, 37, 42-43

Literacy, 42-43

Measurement: of innovativeness, 18, 42, 67, 78, 83-84, 99; issues in defining adoption, 19-20; recall data, 19-20

Mechanization, 58-60, 115, 129

Network analysis, 109-111, 118; historical analysis, 111, 113

North Central Rural Sociology Committee, 21, 22, 24, 37

Ogburn, William F., 3-4, 11

Opinion leaders, 110

Organization innovativeness, 124

Re-invention, 113; defined, 131; selective adoption, 131, 132

Research methodology: of anthropologists, 87; case studies, 118, 119; of economists, 87; ex ante designs, 96, 98, 100; experimental design, 5, 93; ex post designs, 96; meta-research, 80; participatory, 122, 127, 130; process research, 111; of rural sociologists, 79-81, 85-87, 88, 91, 99, 100, 101, 103, 107; sample survey, 1, 5, 10, 48, 79-80, 82, 86-87, 100, 111, 113, 114, 118, 122, 123, 132; variance research, 111

Index

About the Authors

FREDERICK C. FLIEGEL was Professor of Rural Sociology at the University of Illinois. He was the former editor of *Rural Sociology* and the most frequently published author in that journal. He died in 1987 while serving as an international development adviser in Pakistan.

PETER F. KORSCHING is Professor of Sociology at Iowa State University. He has conducted and published extensive basic and applied research on the adoption and diffusion of innovations. He served as director of the North Central Regional Center for Rural Development from 1984-1994.

Social Ecology Press

Environmental, Natural Resource Social Science Books

A CONCEPTUAL APPROACH TO SOCIAL IMPACT ASSESS-
MENT Collection of Writings by Rabel J. Burdge and Colleagues,
by Rabel J. Burdge, Revised Edition — 1998 ....$19.95

A COMMUNITY GUIDE TO SOCIAL IMPACT ASSESSMENT
Revised Edition — 1999 by Rabel J. Burdge $18.95

RURAL SOCIOLOGY AND THE ENVIRONMENT
by Donald R. Field and William R. Burch, Jr. $15.00

Classics in Rural Sociology:

DAYDREAMS AND NIGHTMARES: A SOCIOLOGICAL ESSAY
ON THE AMERICAN ENVIRONMENT —republished in 1998
by William R. Burch, Jr $15.00

DIFFUSION RESEARCH IN RURAL SOCIOLOGY
The Record and Prospects for the Future—republished in 2001
by FREDERICK C. FLIEGEL
with PETER F. KORSCHING $15.00

THE COMMUNITY IN RURAL AMERICA—republished in 1999
by Kenneth P. Wilkinson...$15.00

THREE IRON MINING TOWNS: A STUDY IN CULTURAL
CHANGE by Paul H. Landis—republished in 1999 ... ...$15.00

MAN, MIND AND LAND—republished in 1999
by Walter Firey $15.00

Send orders to: Social Ecology Press
                      P.O. Box 620863
                      Middleton, WI 53562-0863, U.S.A.

(Prices of books and shipping subject to change.)

sterCard, and American Express accepted.

bout larger orders, alternative and foreign shipping.

d FAX (608) 831-1410; Toll Free in U.S. (888) 364-3277

field@dog-eared.com

15: http://www.dog-eared.com/socialecologypress

About the Authors

FREDERICK C. FLIEGEL was Professor of Rural Sociology at the University of Illinois. He was the former editor of *Rural Sociology* and the most frequently published author in that journal. He died in 1987 while serving as an international development adviser in Pakistan.

PETER F. KORSCHING is Professor of Sociology at Iowa State University. He has conducted and published extensive basic and applied research on the adoption and diffusion of innovations. He served as director of the North Central Regional Center for Rural Development from 1984-1994.

Social Ecology Press

Environmental, Natural Resource Social Science Books

A CONCEPTUAL APPROACH TO SOCIAL IMPACT ASSESS-
MENT Collection of Writings by Rabel J. Burdge and Colleagues,
by Rabel J. Burdge, Revised Edition — 1998 ....$19.95

A COMMUNITY GUIDE TO SOCIAL IMPACT ASSESSMENT
Revised Edition — 1999 by Rabel J. Burdge $18.95

RURAL SOCIOLOGY AND THE ENVIRONMENT
by Donald R. Field and William R. Burch, Jr. $15.00

Classics in Rural Sociology:

DAYDREAMS AND NIGHTMARES: A SOCIOLOGICAL ESSAY
ON THE AMERICAN ENVIRONMENT —republished in 1998
by William R. Burch, Jr $15.00

DIFFUSION RESEARCH IN RURAL SOCIOLOGY
The Record and Prospects for the Future—republished in 2001
by FREDERICK C. FLIEGEL
with PETER F. KORSCHING $15.00

THE COMMUNITY IN RURAL AMERICA—republished in 1999
by Kenneth P. Wilkinson...$15.00

THREE IRON MINING TOWNS: A STUDY IN CULTURAL
CHANGE by Paul H. Landis—republished in 1999 ... ...$15.00

MAN, MIND AND LAND—republished in 1999
by Walter Firey $15.00

Send orders to: Social Ecology Press
                         P.O. Box 620863
                         Middleton, WI 53562-0863,U.S.A.

(Prices of books and shipping subject to change.)

Visa, MasterCard, and American Express accepted.

Inquire about larger orders, alternative and foreign shipping.

Phone and FAX (608) 831-1410; Toll Free in U.S. (888) 364-3277

E-mail: field@dog-eared.com

Web Site: http://www.dog-eared.com/socialecologypress